# Designing for
# Interdependence

# DESIGNING IN DARK TIMES

Responding to the current and wide ranging systemic, social, economic, political and environmental challenges we face, the aim of this series is to bring together short, polemical texts that address these crises and their inherent possibilities.

Understanding that the old division between the theoretical focus of the social sciences and the practical stance integral to designing, making and shaping the world is dissolving, *Designing in Dark Times* explores new ways of acting and knowing concerning the artificial. Identified by the refusal of resignation to what-is and by the equal necessity and urgency of developing new models of the possible, the series presents both modes of thought (models, concepts, arguments) and courses of action (scenarios, strategies, proposals, works) at all levels from the local and the micro (the situation) to the global and the macro.

The aim is to push the boundaries of both design and thought, to make each more capable of opening genuine possibilities for thinking and acting otherwise and thus of better facing, and facing down, the myriad failures of the present.

As the world descends into crisis these books seek to offer, in small ways, a counter view. Against the instrumental they use the fact that design is *also* a means of articulating hitherto unforeseen possibilities—for subjects as much as for the world—to show how at base it offers irreplaceable capabilities for thinking and acting well in the artificial. In so doing, they point us towards ways of reversing some of the negative and destructive tendencies threatening to engulf the world.

Clive Dilnot
Eduardo Staszowski

"This life-affirming book advances the field of design engaged with decentering humans and proposes a focus on designing for ecological interdependence. Ávila seamlessly converses between complex theoretical perspectives and concrete design practices. This results in a book that offers both profound reflections on designing relationally and in response to other entities as well as a rich repertoire of examples inspiring practitioners to attune to multispecies worlds. This work takes design in an exciting direction that offers plenty of possibilities to construct alternative futures."

MICHELLE WESTERLAKEN, *Cambridge University*

"In our climate emergency, it's become a truism that we can't solve problems with the same thinking that created them. New thinking is desperately needed. In Martín Ávila's *Designing for Interdependence* new concepts flourish. Rather than mere opposition to a human-centered design paradigm, Ávila carefully incorporates into design key ideas drawn from the field of biosemiotics and from the "biocentric" turn of law and philosophy in Latin and South America. This is made tangible through examples as diverse as designs for urban bee habitats and for co-existing with scorpions. Avila's propositions are welcome and urgent: we need to rethink design as a crucial form of relation to multiple ecologies and biodiversity."

RAMIA MAZÉ, *University of the Arts London*

# Designing for Interdependence: A Poetics of Relating

Martín Ávila

BLOOMSBURY VISUAL ARTS
LONDON • NEW YORK • OXFORD • NEW DELHI • SYDNEY

BLOOMSBURY VISUAL ARTS
Bloomsbury Publishing Plc
50 Bedford Square, London, WC1B 3DP, UK
1385 Broadway, New York, NY 10018, USA
29 Earlsfort Terrace, Dublin 2, Ireland

BLOOMSBURY, BLOOMSBURY VISUAL ARTS and the Diana logo are
trademarks of Bloomsbury Publishing Plc

First published in Great Britain 2022

For legal purposes the Acknowledgements on p. xiv constitute an
extension of this copyright page.

Cover design by Andrew LeClair and Chris Wu of Wkshps

A catalogue record for this book is available from the British Library.

Library of Congress Cataloging-in-Publication Data

Names: Ávila, Martín, 1972– author.
Title: Designing for interdependence : a poetics of relating / Martín Ávila.
Description: London ; New York : Bloomsbury Visual Arts, 2022. | Series: Designing in dark times |
Includes bibliographical references and index.
Identifiers: LCCN 2022013400 (print) | LCCN 2022013401 (ebook) | ISBN 9781350337381 (paperback) |
ISBN 9781350183742 (hardback) | ISBN 9781350183759 (pdf) | ISBN 9781350183766 (epub)
Subjects: LCSH: Design–Environmental aspects. | Sustainable design.
Classification: LCC NK1520 .A95 2022 (print) | LCC NK1520 (ebook) |
DDC 745.401dc23/eng/20220511
LC record available at https://lccn.loc.gov/2022013400
LC ebook record available at https://lccn.loc.gov/2022013401

ISBN:  PB:      978-1-3503-3738-1
       HB:      978-1-3501-8374-2
       ePDF:    978-1-3501-8375-9
       eBook:   978-1-3501-8376-6

Series: Designing in Dark Times

Typeset by RefineCatch Limited, Bungay, Suffolk
Printed and bound in India

To find out more about our authors and books visit www.bloomsbury.com
and sign up for our newsletters.

To Maruca,
Who taught me the patience of soil and the beauty of plants.

# CONTENTS

## FIGURES

# FOREWORD: LIFE DESIGNS FOR FECUNDITY

## Andreas Weber

Design might well be one of the most human-centered practices in this incredibly human-centered epoch, the "Anthropocene". Design mostly serves the goal of selling more products to consumers. New products are often only different in their external shape but keep the same internal components as the last generation (like many cars or consumer audio); the different and presumedly "more modern" design is nothing but a trick to entice buyers into spending.

So mainstream design often follows a one-way route. It is one of the least mutuality-oriented practices our culture hosts. It is presumedly about "beauty"—at least about "good shape"— but what this is about is ultimately decided by the buyer, by those who have more money than others and can afford to follow the fashions of the industry. As Ávila poignantly observes, "Lamps, chairs, telephones, kettles, and most of what populates an average home in any city have been designed in places such as Milan, to be manufactured in places such as Shenzhen, to be used (and discarded) in places such as Guayaquil."

Seen from this angle, design increases the death zone of this planet, which is increasing at breathtaking speed anyway. And designers should stop that. Although the quote from the book's third chapter points to transactions among humans, Ávila goes a big step further: He understands that interdependence is not a human affair alone, but the defining feature of the web of life which we, and human designs, are part and parcel of.

In order to suggest ways of designing which are life-giving (instead of life-taking, as is capitalism as such), we need to design not for consumption, but for life. And this life is not human alone but shared with all other-than-human beings. From this perspective, designing follows a totally different goal: It becomes creation that enables more relations. And only if the broader reciprocity with life as such is respected by what we call design, will the human inhabitants of Guayaquil be treated fairly.

Ávila draws together the bulk of avantgarde theory which is currently discovering that the world is neither "just discourse", the play of the signifiers, nor dead matter, the work of numbers and deterministic laws of "nature". It is "intra-action", continuous meeting and probing. Every meeting "matters", as expresses the physicist and feminist philosopher Karen Barad, one of the core witnesses of Ávila's project. The world as such is shared, it is a commons created and maintained by all beings, and through this sharing alone it comes alive, and develops the manifold perspectives we experience as individualities.

If we design well, we design for this shared aliveness. We create with the goal that the affordances for more encounters created through our design matter—but matter not only in the sense of glory and attention, a rising tide for the designer's ego and wallet, but matter in the sense that the world becomes richer in depth and fecundity. This is the original function of the design that was there before any designer: The evolutionary pathways of the biosphere which create ever more ways of relating, ever more, to speak in the words of Charles Darwin, "endless forms most beautiful".

Andreas Weber is a biologist, philosopher and nature writer. Author of a number of books including *Enlivenment* (MIT Press, Cambridge, 2019) he is Adjunct Professor at the Indian Institute of Technology and teaches at Bard College, Berlin and at the Gastronomic University, Pollenzo, Italy.

# ACKNOWLEDGMENTS

This book is the result of a drafting period of about four years, that started in 2017 but which collects work carried out since 2009. As such, it grew out of being in dialogue with numerous people; with friends, colleagues, and students in many places, and by engaging in experimental design work carried out in collaboration. During this period I have been fortunate to benefit from help, advice, participation, and support from many, including Jenny Althoff, Jimena Arrechederreta, Silvia Barei, Lourdes Boero, Otto von Busch, Ana Calviño, Diego Combina, Henrik Ernstson, Fernando Filippi, Fabian Gallucci, Gerardo Funes, Pernilla Glaser, Guillermo Hilas, Daniel Igarzabal, Mahmoud Keshavarz, Kalevi Kull, Thomas Laurien, Gerardo Leynaud, Petra Lilja, Mariano Lucia, Alejandro Marcella, Camilo Mattoni, José Manuel Meriles, Katja Pettersson, Anna Maria Orrù, Beto Peralta, Rubén Ravera, Johan Redström, Erik Sandelin, Alfredo Sattler, Magali Supo, John Thackara, Mariel Twentyman, Peter Ullmark, Stina Wessman, and Bo Westerlund. In very different ways, they have contributed to make this book and its work possible, better, or both.

I would also like to express my gratitude to Konstfack, the School or Arts, Crafts and Design, for the research time at work in 2018 and 2019 that allowed me to create the necessary "bubbles" to immerse myself in the writing of this book. As usual, everyone at Konstfack's library, has been supportive through the different stages of this project, your dedication and generosity are very much appreciated.

I have also received funding from The Swedish Research Council (project diary number: 438-2013-297) which financed the years of postdoctoral work of "Symbiotic tactics" (2013–2016) and the opportunity to collaborate with researchers at the Multidisciplinary Institute of Vegetal Biology of Córdoba, Argentina (IMBIV). This has been a fantastic collaboration and I would like to thank Gabriel Bernardello for the invaluable support and the opening of so many doors that engaged me in the worlds of ecologists, biologists, activists, and more.

I am very thankful to the undisclosed reviewers of the book in its drafting process. I have certainly made efforts to respond—

which I hope you will recognize in this printed and final version—to the careful and constructive observations made which led to the maturing of several of the early positions of the draft. Special thanks to Clive Dilnot who, in his role as editor, provided invaluable guidance through the drafting of this book. Clive's patience, dedication, and constructive criticism have allowed me to grow by helping me to be more articulate, to make more sense to myself and to others.

The projects of Chapter 2 have all been developed in collaboration with my friend and colleague Leonardo López. Even though the framings have come from my own research initiatives, Leo's thinking and doing are as present as mine throughout the book.

Lastly, without the loving support of my family, in Sweden, Argentina, and other parts of the world, this publication would not be possible, as always you are my stable ground, the more necessary in these unstable times. A special, loving thank-you to my partner Kajsa Öberg Ávila for being there then, and here now, with me.

Relation is the knowledge in motion of beings, which risks the being of the world.

*Poetics of Relation*, ÉDOUARD GLISSANT

# Introduction: Bio-centric?

> These movements of mine, my language calls them by
> the same name: emotions. I am therefore recounting
> my emotions when they encounter the emotions of
> other bodies and the emotions of the Biogea.
> *Biogea*, MICHEL SERRES

## THE PIGEONS

One morning on my way to work, I stepped out of the house through the side door that led to the garage, and as I was about to start my motorbike, I saw that on a plant on the windowsill, a mother pigeon had three nestlings. I took the camera that I was always carrying with me at that time and took the photo that you see below (Figure 0.1). I still remember my first impression: Wow, life finds its ways! And then, almost immediately, well, *that* life, the life of the pigeons, but how about the life of the plant that is in the pot? I did not want to look too close not to scare the pigeons, but I knew that several others were there too; the spiders on the plants and walls and some wasps that had built a nest that was hanging there, to name the few that I could directly see with my own eyes.

And so, a simple idea struck me; could I design a pot that would better accommodate a few of those creatures? Maybe not all the creatures, just the pigeons, the spiders, and the plant? Knowing that pigeons return to the same nesting place, it could look like a terraced pot with cavities on the walls, enough to

host those that I had just seen . . . as I left home, those thoughts
faded away and other priorities came up. I never pursued the
project, at that time I was working with colleagues, studying
different native plant and animal species of that region, some of
which were not as easy to sympathize with as the pigeons, such
as scorpions that get into households through the gratings of
bathrooms. However, the idea I was pursuing through these
projects was the same one: to design things that are less anthropocentric and more hospitable to other life forms. In all cases,
one of the challenges was—as in the relation of the pigeons and
the plant on the pot—how to materialize something that would
engage a person in activities which could also benefit several
species?[1] A design which, through its configuration, would recognize and be attentive to human social and cultural differences,
without diminishing ecological complexity. A design which,
through its configuration, would strive for long-term cohabitation even under circumstances where competition for food or
territory may be at stake.

This book is an exploration of some of the challenges and
possibilities of conceiving design practices based on premises
for cohabitation of human and other-than-human species. We
will be paying attention to the signifying dimensions of design[2]
to help devise processes that can attune to the perceptual capacities of other-than-human beings. We may be asking: What signs

---

[1] From the outset, it is important to understand the category of "species" in
its dynamism, relationality, and fluidity. The word is a shorthand that
acknowledges that "species" is based on family resemblances and is a
category that is fundamentally blurry, fuzzy. See Kull (2016). See also Donna
Haraway's comments of species as formed by a "four-part composition, in
which co-constitution, finitude, impurity, historicity, and complexity are
what is." Haraway (2003: 16).

[2] I will be elaborating upon bio/ecosemiotic approaches to signification
throughout the book. Without attempting a historical review, in the context
of industrial design, explicit attention to semiosis, as the study of signification, has been made for almost a century. See Gay and Samar (1994).
Semiosis was explicitly part of Tomás Maldonado's influence on the Ulm
school of design, and students at Ulm such as Gui Bonsiepe and Klaus
Krippendorff where heavily influenced by these ideas. See for example

FIGURE 0.1  Pigeons on a pot. (Photo by author)

are there to allow some to use certain things in certain ways? What patterns and regularities are recognised and tapped into? By whom? For example, is the pigeon adopting the pot by following a behavioural pattern that we are not recognizing or not caring to recognize? Do humans like me buy pots to put plants on windowsills because we find the plants beautiful or useful? Are these patterns making differences to others? If so, which others and in what way? And through such questions approach the tensions of interspecies cohabitation.

How much in conflict are the actions of the humans, the pigeons, the spiders, and the plants in this case? What is clear is that there are things at stake in these mundane everyday acts; the pot, made of plastic, will at some point be discarded, no longer affecting the life of the plant and the birds but some other ecosystem and those that participate in it. Will it become part of a new industrial cycle by being recycled and converted

Krippendorff (2006) and some of the essays in Bonsiepe (2021) Yet, none of the earlier approaches attempt to account for a multispecies approach such as this book proposes.

into something else? Will it be disposed of and contaminate a water flows or the soil somewhere? By exploring the material agency of things in relation to all kinds of beings, humans included, a poetics of relating emerges, one that grounds the signs of our material culture through shared ecological realities. There are design ecologies and ecologies of designing that maintain or attend to certain things while ignoring or disattending others.

In the overlap between the recognition of multispecies worlds and the re-cognition of design as a signifying activity across species, this book is about the reworking of a dominant material culture that has become synonymous with consumption (product design)[3], and thus with ecological devastation. For this reason, it is an effort to conceive alternative artefacts (or rather, as will be developed in the coming chapters, artefacts as *alter-natives*), through a critical approach of consumer-driven narratives, proposing instead design which engages in place-making to scaffold biodiversity.

## COMPOSING A TITLE

Like most books, this one has been the result of years of (interrupted) drafting. During this course, it has changed titles a few times, and as suggested by a reviewer at an earlier editorial phase, it was called "Biocentric Designing," which was the working title until the later part of the writing process. After a period of processing, we decided to change the title back to an earlier and now final proposition: *Designing for Interdependence: A Poetics of Relating*. I will unpack the issues and nuances in the choosing of the title since I believe that it will help clarifying not only the title, but the topic and the arguments of this book.

One of the reasons for this change is that I prefer not to use words that qualify the word design, as in "speculative design," "experience design," "transition design," and so on. I believe that

[3] In this way, this book intends to complement but also often argue against the well-intended and predominantly anthropocentric product design discourse about "sustainability." See for example Penty (2019).

design always has degrees of all kinds of actions (speculation upon some issues, experiential dimensions, proposals for transitions into some things and not others, etc.). I had accepted "biocentric designing" as a working title since I could be in peace with the word design*ing*, with an emphasis on process, and therefore it could indicate the striving towards biocentrism, rather than the achievement of it. However, although I was using the word "biocentric," this word was also problematic to me, for a range of reasons, but perhaps more importantly, by the simple fact that the word "bio" was coupled with the word "centre."

*Biocentrism* is not a new conception, it has legacies that can be traced back decades, and is anchored on insights that are centuries old or even millenarian depending on the perspective adopted, as is the case if we understand biocentrism under certain cosmologies or traditional ecological knowledges. It overlaps with other conceptions such as ecocentrism or ecosophy, to name two prominent strands, yet the meaning of the word "bios" has drawn philosophical attention in relation to a potential legacy that links it tightly not with life in general but with human life in particular. This is problematic since the concept of biocentrism attempts to "de-centre" the human and have no "centre" or if one could speak of a centre, as the word suggests, it would be life itself as centre. The debate has to do with the Greek legacy of the word *bios* which signifies "life," yet another word was also used to designate the living by the Greek: *zōē*. Both words, bios-zōē were distinguished but used ambiguously. In recent years, this distinction has been framed to belong to different spheres of life, on the one hand *bios*, relating to human life and on the other hand *zōē*, relating to everything else that is alive.[4] Building

---

[4] Philosopher Rosi Braidotti writes: "Post-anthropocentrism is marked by the emergence of 'the politics of life itself' (Rose, 2007). 'Life', far from being codified as the exclusive property or the unalienable right of one species, the human, over all others or of being sacralized as a pre-established given, is posited as process, interactive and open-ended. This vitalist approach to living matter displaces the boundary between the portion of life—both organic and discursive—that has traditionally been reserved for *anthropos*, that is to say *bios*, and the wider scope of animal and non-human life, also known as *zoe. Zoe* as the dynamic, self-organizing structure of life itself

upon these debates on the sovereign role of the human, I was drafting a book using the word biocentrism, striving to capture the life–death and biotic–abiotic *continuum* that characterizes "life" in our planet, *without* the distinctions between *bios* and *zōē*. But I could not quite undo the connotations of *bios*. I had started to use the concept of biocentrism by aligning with the so-called "biocentric turn" in Latin America, which gave rights to "nature" and resulted in the change of constitutions in Bolivia and Ecuador, and as such, an approach to understand citizenship and forms of belonging to the places we inhabit through Andean cosmologies[5]. In relation to the field of systems ecology, biocentrism also aligns with research in biocultural diversity, which has developed from a "crisis narrative" to a "dynamic narrative" that studies the dynamics of people and environments, whether these are urban ecologies or others.[6] The confluences of these fields of study and practices still inform and are relevant to the proposals of this book.

But in spite of this, it was the word "centre" that remained cumbersome. When we say "biocentric" we are referring to putting "life at the centre of consideration" or a centre that is everywhere, distributed. This is quite straightforward, yet it is necessary to specify in what way there is no "centre" and why the word "centre" both in anthropo*centrism* and bio*centrism* is problematic.

(Braidotti 2006; 2011b) stands for generative vitality. It is the transversal force that cuts across and reconnects previously segregated species, categories and domains. *Zoe*-centred egalitarianism is, for me, the core of the post-anthropocentric turn: it is a materialist, secular, grounded and unsentimental response to the opportunistic trans-species commodification of Life that is the logic of advanced capitalism." (Braidotti 2013: 60). Laurent Dubreuil's etymological and philological investigation of ancient Greek works in relation to the writings of Giorgio Agamben and Roberto Esposito, asserts that bios-zōē were distinguished but used ambiguously even by single authors such as Aristotle or Plato. In this sense, Braidotti continues the distinctions set forth by Agamben and Esposito. See Dubreuil (2006: 83–98).

[5] See Gudynas (2014).

[6] See Elands, Vierikko, Andersson, Fischer, Gonçalves, Haase, et al. (2019). In relation to design see also Davidson-Hunt, Turner, Pareake Mead, Cabrera-Lopez, BoltonIdrobo, et al. (2012).

If we start with anthropocentrism, not all *anthropos* (the generic name for our human species) enacts worlds through the same practices and relate to the living in the same way. Quite the opposite, examples across the planet as well as much scholarship tell of the immense contemporary as well as historical disparity human communities have and have had in relation to "nature."[7] As it is well known, most of us living in the so-called Global North not only consume most and are directly responsible for most pollution, but also continue to adopt lifestyles that are based on colonial and oppressive patterns of different kind.[8] The "centre" in anthropocentrism cannot be assumed as a given in a universal way, but always needs to be contextualized relationally, contingently. The fussy category *anthropos*, like the fussy category *species*, points at beings that are multiple, complex, queer, dynamic. In spite of this, as Rosi Braidotti notes, the legacy and connotations of anthropocentrism resonate with the figure of the human as male, white, Eurocentric being, producing an othering in relation to "the sexualized other (woman), the racialized other (the native) and the naturalized other (animals, the environment or earth)," also in opposition to the technological artefact.[9]

The "centre" in anthropo*centrism* is also problematic because "we" so-called individuals (humans) are far from being "singular," rather we are "plural" and "multiple," enacted by ecologies of bacteria, flows of minerals and gases and permanently and contingently dependent on the environments which we inhabit. Yet, following a relational and ecological approach, it therefore makes sense to speak about creating practices that displace the "centre" in anthropocentrism because the figure of *anthropos*

[7] In the context of design see for example Fallan (2019). Also, Watson (2020).

[8] See for example Plumwood (2002); Mignolo (2011); Yusoff (2018); Santos, and Meneses, (2014). In the design context, Escobar (2018); Boehnert (2018).

[9] See Braidotti (2013: 26–27). Also "The human norm stands for normality, normalcy and normativity. It functions by transposing a specific mode of being human into a generalized standard, which acquires transcendent values as *the* human: from male to masculine and onto human as the universalized format of humanity." (26).

of which we speak here is the very conception of the human as an independent, autonomous being capable of mastering "nature" instead of *being* "nature." What needs to be established instead is the conception of the human as an interdependent creature enacted relationally and inseparably from the thermodynamic and metabolic flows of the biosphere.[10]

This understanding of *inter*dependence is partly what makes problematic the "centre" in bio*centrism*. The word biocentrism has a metaphorical dimension that "gathers" a poetic image, which captures the insight that life is possible in the bio*sphere*. The term biosphere describes the "zone of life on earth" and works in analogy with the spherical shape of the planet we inhabit. Humans and pigeons and plants and spiders live, and thus are part of the biosphere, of what we call life, the living. But in the biosphere hierarchies appear: some feed on others, or some convert the energy from the sun that provide the basis for the rest of the living, to give two fundamental examples of food chains. This means that there are myriad forms of agency, with extremely different capacities to affect and enact the biosphere, no "centre" is to be found but a multiplicity of intra-actions[11] enacting the whole. In both senses therefore, the word "centre" has a metaphoric clang that we have to remain attentive to, in order to avoid universalizing claims about any phenomena: social, cultural, biological, or ecological.

[10] See Schneider and Sagan (2005); Margulis and Sagan (2007).

[11] Physicist Karen Barad coined the term *intra-action* to explain (explicate) the related influencing of "things." Intra-action is a dynamic concept (to be understood in terms of processes) that emphasizes agency, not as an inherent property of a thing or an individual (which might be taken for granted through the notion of inter-action) but as relational becoming. "Agency is not an attribute but the ongoing reconfigurings of the world" writes Barad. See Barad (2007: 141). Through this conception, "things" are ethico-onto-epistemologically constitutive of each other. We are always in the middle. I will develop this position through the contingentist approach of biologist Kriti Sharma (2015). An account of the agency of things can be found in Bennett (2010). An exploration of the perception of spheres in relation to environmental issues can be found in Ingold (2000: 209–218).

To add to this list of cautions, some debates on biocentrism tend towards forms of anti-anthropocentrism, claiming the recognition of the value of all life by equating humans to every other form of life. To me, this is problematic since it does not acknowledge the power differentials and the agency of different species, particularly the human species. There are inter-species dynamics with conflict of interests such as territorial or prey–predator relations, all affecting complex ecological systems, and there are also intra-species hierarchies and power dimensions that maintain whole populations in certain dynamics. Following this logic, the best conception of biocentrism would mean to better understand human worlds, to be even more anthropocentric if you like, valuing all life but not claiming a flattening of hierarchies, as it is fundamental to make explicit and understand hierarchies in ecosystems as in geopolitics. Whether we want it or not, humans have become dominant species, but this dominance plays out very differently, therefore, to aim at making this power transparent or visible preserves the possibility of accountability and responsibility.

This is not a way however to reintroduce human exceptionalism through the back door and make human benefit the final parameter to conceive relations to other beings.

Throughout this book, the striving for life-affirmation implies the "de-centring" of humans, which through the practice of design attempts to add ethical and political accountability towards other lives, yet humans differ and various degrees of anthropocentrism and relations to environments enact very different naturecultures.[12] Because of this, life affirmation should not be understood as a specific form of "centring" around a universal human even less privileging certain biopolitical lives. If we may call it biocentrism, it is a biocentrism that implies ontological perspectivism[13] and

---

[12] Donna Haraway started using the term natureculture in *The Companion Species Manifesto*. Haraway emphasises the becoming-with in "sympoisesis" and proposes the term "holoents" to replace "units" or "beings" to capture the relational, dynamic and queer aspects of living. See Haraway (2016: 60–61).

[13] See Viveiros de Castro (2014). Also, Latour (2013).

no unitarian suggestion of an Anthropocene with capital A, rather "a billion black anthropocenes," acknowledging colonial history and current forms of oppression.[14]

I have been emphasizing the relationality and entanglement of the biotic–abiotic, which forms a continuum in which the artificial[15] is part. Following this reasoning, another challenge with the word biocentrism is that if it is not interpreted as life-centric in a general way, but only as life-centric in the specific sense of focusing on organisms, on what are described as sentient beings, then the approach may turn problematic by being primarily concerned with animals and perhaps insects, while backgrounding plants, the mineral world, abiotic processes, and things created by humans. In this sense, what I have been describing and what I will continue to present may be closer to definitions of "ecocentrism" and more particularly to the ecosophy proposed by psychiatrist, philosopher, and activist Félix Guattari, as will be developed in the following chapters.

As a result of these considerations, I will use the word ecocentrism to indicate the difference with anthropocentrism, yet much of what is discussed in the coming pages owes to the development of ideas of biocentric approaches and so the work stands on the overlaps of discourses, without making sharp distinctions between the so-called biocentrism and ecocentrism. What this framing does not authorise though, is a reading of this approach as an idealised vision of harmony with "nature," at least not if harmony stands for a frictionless conviviality. This

[14] Kathryn Yusoff makes explicit the connection between geology and colonialism by enacting what she calls *White Geology*. "In twining the traffic between the human and inhumane, the presumed neutrality of geology as a mode of description is disrupted. Blackness is displaced and effaced in the pursuit of value for Western colonialism through and as extraction. Geologic principles are used to establish a biocentrism that delineates from the human to subhuman to inhuman, as a property relation and as a mark of agentic properties. It is not that geology is productive of race per se but that empirical processes mesh across geological propositions and propositions of racial identity to produce an equation of inhuman property as racially coded." (2018: 73). A design industry complicit of the extraction and consumption of minerals participates in these forms of colonial patterns.
[15] Regarding what we call artificial, see Dilnot (2015) and also Dilnot (2021).

book is instead about cultivating affective ecologies across species, where design makes a difference and is based on a coherence grounded on biophysical constraints.

In terms of design, this requires first, that designed artefacts tune in to other-than-human perceptual capacities and ways of worldmaking; second, that through the creation of material cultures that embody interspecies care[16] aim to increase abilities to cohabit. This also requires that, collectively (in multiple collectives) the designed artefacts are conceived and realized/created with precautionary principles, i.e., with an understanding that all manner of beings will relate to the devices we create. There are always issues at stake when rearranging and reconfiguring the places that we live, friction is constantly enacted even when cooperation may be the aim. I can increase the number of pots that may host not only plants but also pigeons yet, negatively affect the possibilities of endemic species to feed, or multiple other occurrences that may emerge from the presence of the birds, the plants, and the pots.

It is for all these reasons that the working title "Biocentric Designing" was replaced by *Designing for Interdependence*. In this shift, the word *designing* remained, but it was not qualified by any other word, and was linked with a new emphasis in the title on "interdependence."

As mentioned earlier, the phrasing of design as design*ing* was important, a striving towards understanding designing always as *process*. The activity we call design is a form of response, a response that is enacted by the capacity to adapt to different environments and transform them at some scale to our (human) benefit or our liking. The use of "ing" in design*ing*, indicates "in the making", and the importance to conceive these artefacts as processes, as becoming, as particular crystallizations and sedimentations of specific socio-ecological conditions which are never static but dynamic, both socially and ecologically. Through these precautions and nuances, we are approaching part of what is at stake in the word I added, *interdependence*: the mutual

---

[16] See Puig de la Bellacasa (2017).

constitution of things. What does this entail? In her book *Interdependence*, biologist Kriti Sharma writes,

> the ascendant view of interdependence at play in biology—as in popular culture—is *not a view of interdependence at all*. It remains a view of *independence*. By and large, we think that interdependence just means "*independent* objects *interacting*." We say that things interact strongly, weakly, reciprocally, sequentially, and so on, but their ultimate independence from one another remains intact.[17]

Sharma asserts that there is a transition being made, and that therefore there is a necessary "shift from considering things in isolation to considering things in interaction" arguing that "a second shift is required: one from considering things in interaction to considering things as *mutually constituted*, that is, viewing things as existing at all only due to the dependence on other things."[18] This is what Sharma calls "contingentism." Something is contingent when it depends upon its existence on something else, and we can practice this thinking and understanding by constantly asking the question "What does this depend on?"[19]

At the moment of writing these words, "I" depend upon many things that make my body not totally distinguishable from its surrounding environment. We depend upon things that we normally take for granted, for example, I depend upon the air that I am constantly breathing, and the water and food that I previously ingested, which form part of my metabolism. In a real sense these not only "maintain" but constantly "create" me. If the air that I breathe did not have oxygen, a series of processes would lead to my collapse within minutes and "my" relations to the "environment" would change radically. Needless to say, that the amount of oxygen in the air depends upon plants of all kinds producing it through photosynthesis, which in turn are dependent upon myriad processes that we cannot take for granted. May pots for

[17] See Sharma (2015: 1–2 emphasis in the original).
[18] Sharma (2015: 2).
[19] Sharma (2015: 103).

plants be a way to make oxygen available in some environments? What do pots depend on? What do pigeons depend on?

Following chains of interdependencies, this book is mostly concerned with *ecological interdependence*,[20] putting emphasis on the mutual dependencies that make life possible. The dependencies of soil and plants and sun to enact the first steps in so-called food chains, since plants are eaten by herbivores who in turn are eaten by carnivores, who in turn, once they die, become food to decomposers and microbes, making available nutrients to soils and plants, continuing the cycles of regeneration. Dependencies of living with non-living entities. Through these processes, we bring forth worlds by living,[21] and understanding the worlds brought forth by humans is crucial to become articulate about the enaction of what is natural for humans to produce: the artificial. Yet, as we will explore throughout the book, the dominant culture of the artificial does not participate in the lifecycles of most beings, enacting destructive patterns which are not conductive to the affirmation of life.

Looking at relations that design cultures and designed things create with other creatures, we will be paying attention to how not only humans, but other living non-human beings may attribute meaning to the designed things they encounter, since they depend just as much as humans, on interpreting habitats for their own constitution and for their survival.

Yet, the title *Designing for Interdependence* may still seem redundant, we *are* interdependent, there is *no choice*, why would we need to design for interdependence? The short answer is, to undo the perception of humans as independent creatures detached from environments and other beings, and thus, to change the

[20] Sharma distinguishes among ecological interdependence, regulatory interdependence, hierarchical interdependence, and ontological interdependence. See, Sharma (2015: 102–103).
[21] See Maturana and Varela (1998). The enactive approach to cognition of Maturana and Varela forms part of what Sharma describes as contingentism. See Sharma (2015: 101–103). See also Chapter 2 where "world" is elaborated in relation to Jakob von Uexküll's "Umwelt" based on Francisco Varela's distinctions of world and environment.

paradigm of design from anthropocentric to ecocentric, and to change design practices from extractive and exploitative to life-affirming.


## DESIGN, CONTROL

By challenging anthropocentrism through design, a practice emerges from questioning human mastery, and thus a poetics of relating is developed by means of a letting go of control acknowledging other-than-human needs and capacities. In this sense this book is about control, at least to the extent that a human can let go of control by designing something that affirms her living.

Designed artefacts trigger responses from those that encounter them, whether those that come in contact with these are human or not. Since most designs have been devised keeping (some) human beings in mind, what these artefacts tend to "control" (trigger, mediate), are the capacities and possibilities of (some) humans to respond to the environment in particular ways that benefit them. For example, even though a brick wall for a house gets in contact with all kinds of beings, it has been devised to include humans and their preferences (as much as this technology affords) and exclude others considered threatening (to the humans or the house itself) such as spiders, fungi, tigers, or whatever may be "outside" of that "inside" and controlled environment. Control is key to make sure that things function properly. Much effort, for example, goes to designing the many parts that make the door of a car close smoothly (read "in a controlled way"). Yet, by attending to human needs only, we focus on a very thin spectrum of the living, and this has immense and devastating ecological repercussions. Imagine that the car door that we are speaking about is made of metal, how does the extraction of metal relate to the living in the places where it is extracted? How about all the intermediary phases in the whole of the life-cycle of this artefact? From extraction to discard and eventual recycling, how does the manufacturing processes that result in a metal door relate to other living beings that are not the primary users of the car, human or not? These are fundamental questions in this book. They shape a *political ecology of the artificial*.

Throughout this book, the word design is not limited to any field of design, such as product design, interaction design, architecture, or graphic design, but encompasses the general capacity to adapt to and transform environments, which in turn triggers adaption to those beings participating in the environments. In short, design is a general form of human response that results in the transformation of environments. In this book most examples of "design" will be of three-dimensional artefacts that we normally call "products," things that have been conceived to perform a specific function. I use these examples to reflect on the current dominant culture of artefacts that is typically called industrial or product design.

The book does not expand on established areas of expertise such as biomimicry or cradle to cradle processes, which form part of the emergent horizon of ecological awareness and are fundamental to continue with for the refinement of our understanding of coevolutionary and adaptive processes.[22] Yet, the poetics of relating of this book are a mode of resistance to the dominant industrial inertia, and an active resistance to the anthropocentrism of the current design paradigm. Something may participate in a circular economy, which may contribute to industrial or biological cycles following cradle to cradle principles, yet they may remain anthropocentric and continue to expand material flows (through extractivist practices coupled to financial expansionism) that destroy biodiversity at other scales. Similarly, although biomimicry is "the practice of looking to nature for inspiration to solve design problems in a regenerative way"[23] design propositions that only follow biomimicry principles to imitate the forms of natural phenomena and not their processes,

[22] See Benyus (1997). For resources see: https://asknature.org. About cradle to cradle see MacDonough and Braungart (2002). Organizations such as the Ellen McArthur Foundation or the Cradle to Cradle Institute continue to disseminate and refine the model, see: https://www.ellenmacarthurfoundation.org.

[23] https://biomimicry.org Accessed June 21, 2021.

may result in applications that are toxic and do not participate in the life of the places where they are used, as is the case, for example, with the development of some surface treatments that are hydrophobic, inspired by the microscopic structure of lotus leaves.[24]

Instead, this work approaches design for its capacity to affect and mediate *relations*. An ecological approach is thoroughly relational; what I emphasize is the lack of ecoliteracy[25] in the compositions that we call design, in the lack of ecological awareness through responses to other-than-human beings.

Sometimes, the best response is not to design but to let be. This is more urgent now than at any other time in the history of humanity since the industrial revolution. This is why this book, and its approach should be understood as a complement to conservation efforts. It argues for an ecocentrism through the practice of the artificial that can support the rewilding that needs to happen if we are to contribute to the stabilization of planetary dynamics

---

[24] https://asknature.org/?s=lotus&page=0&hFR%5Bpost_type_ label%5D%5B0%5D=Innovations&is_v=1 Accessed June 21, 2021. See also the findings in the report "Biomimicry in the Nordic Countries" by Anker Lenau, Orrù, and Linkola, (2018). Even the United Nations "Sustainable Development Goals" risk becoming unsustainable, if some of the goals such as number eight "Decent work and economic growth" is not counterbalanced with number 12 "responsible production and consumption." The ground for the goals is number 14 and 15, "life below water" and "life on land" respectively, if we do not understand these ecological constraints the rest of the goals (no poverty, zero hunger, good health and wellbeing, etc.) become unachievable and narrowly anthropocentric. See https://sdgs.un.org/goals. Accessed June 21, 2021

[25] The term ecoliteracy was developed after David Orr's book *Ecological Literacy: Education and the Transition to a Postmodern World* (Orr, 1992). In their book *Ecoliterate* Daniel Goleman, Lisa Bennett and Zenobia Barlow summarize five practices of emotionally and socially engaged ecoliteracy: 1, Developing empathy for all forms of life; 2, Embracing sustainability as a community practice (understanding that organisms do not exist in isolation); 3, Making the invisible visible (effects of human behaviour on other people and the environment); 4, Anticipating unintended consequences (precautionary principles); 5, Understanding how nature sustains life (learn strategies that are applicable to designing human endeavours) (2012: 10). See also Boehnert (2015).

and the affirmation of biodiversity.[26] A designing that makes us
more obviously dependable on other forms of life in its biotic–
abiotic continuum, a designing for interdependence.


## COHABITATION

In the context of the current mass extinction of species across
the planet, conservation work is *essential*. In the year 2014, at
the time when I was working in Argentina on the projects of
"symbiotic tactics", some of which I will show in Chapter 2, only
3–5% of the native forests of the province of Córdoba remained.
The rest had been urbanized or used for agricultural purposes.
In this context, the projects that will be presented are examples
of possibilities to relate through design to humans and other-
than-human beings and are situated within existing spaces already
transformed by direct human intervention such as cities or agricultural fields. These are meant to *complement* the type of
scenarios that many conservationists are suggesting. The projects
are about reconsidering forms of cohabitation with other
than humans, so that the continuum natureculture may become

---

[26] See for example the creative conservation efforts of the Rewilding movement
as described by George Monbiot in *Feral. Rewilding the land, sea and human
life* (Monbiot, 2014). Biologist E. O. Wilson has written that only by setting
aside half the planet in reserve, or more, it is possible to save the living part
of the environment and achieve the stabilization required for human survival.
Wilson's "half-earth" proposal is not only about physical spaces for cohabitation, but also about knowledge, lack of knowledge; "We need a much deeper
understanding of ourselves and the rest of life than the humanities and sciences
have yet offered" (Wilson, 2016: 3). Preserving (or restoring) 50% of a region's
natural habitats is certainly a challenge in any part of the world, and while I
embrace Wilson's suggestion, it must be clear that all areas of the world have
human populations. Conservation is not only a delimitation of territory for
the protection of species or ecosystems, but also about the sustainment of
diverse human-other-than-human forms of cohabitation. The "we" in "we
need a much deeper understanding . . ." from the quote above, points at the
arrogance of the current and dominant anthropocentric and capitalist-industrial
paradigm, not to the multiple indigenous communities that have maintained
ecosystemic balance in the places where they live.

enactive and performative of life-affirming processes. These projects do *not* suggest the possibility of expansion as a mode of engagement in and with environments. They can be seen as ways of thinking and acting intensively rather than extensively, or, in the words of philosopher and biologist Andreas Weber, as ways of increasing "depth," and as complements to the rewilding that has to occur if biodiversity is to be a source of wealth, wonder, and resilience. An expansive culture and economy are quite simply unrealistic in the sense that the paradigm of "expansion" is based on the abstraction of endless "resources" and not of biophysical constraints. In Weber's words:

> The biosphere does not grow. The total quantity of biomass does not increase. The throughput of matter does not expand; nature runs a steady-state economy—that is, an economy in which all relevant factors remain constant in relation to each other. Nor does the number of species necessarily increase; it rises in some epochs and falls in others. The only dimension that really grows is the diversity of experiences: ways of feeling, modes of expression, variations of appearance, novelties in patterns and forms. Therefore, nature gains neither mass nor weight, but rather depth. This is not a dimension that can be evaluated and quantified, however. It is a poetic expression of a sediment of desire that is either frustrated or fulfilled.[27]

Following this thread, it is possible to say that through the mass extinctions humans are generating there is an erasure of this depth, a "shallowness" in nature and experience that is being created systematically and on an everyday basis.[28] A shallowness

[27] Weber (2019: 72).

[28] I would also like to note the metaphoric aspect of the word "depth," which in Weber's case suggests "intensity." But we should be careful to use the word "depth" in contrast to "shallow"; by analogy, most surfaces are considered shallow, but on these surfaces (such as the human skin or the shores of the sea) is where most exchanges happen, where most diversity is to be found and so the idea of "depth" shouldn't be understood in physical but in ecological terms.

generated by production and consumption immersed in an expansionist capitalist-industrial complex, which in its advance undoes the links, erases species with their experience of their habitats and thus undoes their role in enacting and maintaining these habitats.

The poetics of relating pursued here suggest that designing, as a human response, has to play its part and intensify its poetic and configurative expressions to attune to other-than-human ways of knowing and feeling, to create patterns and forms that have the possibility to become life-affirming. To play its part to create the possibility of co-adaptation, of getting on together in the tensions and responsibility of asymmetric power.

To work with design and cohabitation implies the invention and maintenance of material and process cultures based on dynamics of relating that can support biodiversity. What I mean by process cultures, are cultures that perceive themselves a part of living cycles through their social and material production, constantly nurturing the becoming of things that affirm the living in the places where these things happen to be produced, used and discarded. To cohabit is to pattern a (habit) together, a patterning that evolves through mutual adaptation. A patterning that through designs that recognize other beings, accommodate and probe response-abilities[29] of the beings involved. Each being is attuned to the rhythms of the biosphere, of the geosphere, of the cosmos, and enact patterns that are interpreted by those participating and enacting the semiotic entanglement of all these, the semiosphere. In the field of design, Christopher Alexander has pioneered the study of "pattern languages,"[30] as a field that seeks to understand the patterning that humans have created throughout history at different scales and in different ways, as languages that emerge, ranging from material possibilities that afford certain types of patterning, to architectural spaces or urban situations

---

[29] In *Staying with the Trouble*, Haraway develops the notion of response-ability as cultivating knowing and doing, and referring to the work of Isabelle Stengers, as "an ecology of practices" (2016: 34). See also the section "Ecologies" in Chapter 1.

[30] Alexander (1977).

that have triggered certain social behaviour. We can further these and include multimodal approaches by which other-than-human patterning become explicit, allowing for the possibility to understand innumerable overlaps, as will be discussed later in the book.

Life affirmation in this sense is a way to bring to the forefront sentience and the lived experience of beings while partaking in ecologies, which implies participating in exchanges of information (sense making) with other species, as well as connecting these exchanges to the thermodynamic flows by which matter circulates, patterns, and affects cultures, human and other.

## I, WE, US, IT AND OTHERS

In this attempt to act and think less anthropocentrically one is permanently kept in check by the simple fact of being human, that is, by the cognitive and experiential capacities of being human as well as being a cultural version of *anthropos*. In a sentence as the one I wrote describing my initial encounter with the pigeons, "And so, a simple idea struck me; could I design a pot that would better accommodate a few of those creatures that I had already seen?" we can read several things: a belief that as a (human) trained designer, and that through the material culture that "we" are creating, one can offer possibilities of hospitality to other-than-humans; basically, a human assumption that through human artifice things will be "better."

In this assumption (human) vision, physically and as a metaphor, plays an important role: the knowledge that I have about these species is very limited, and as "I see" I am acting by the situation of the mother pigeon with her nestlings, something that affects me emotionally since I project feelings of compassion to those beings whom I can identify with, such as mothers and children, as well as with the need for warmth, feeding, protection, and so on. How anthropocentric of me! But this book does not offer an argument for the possibility to design "non-anthropocentrically." If what we call design is a human activity (as it could be said that a beaver dam has been designed by a beaver), then it is impossible for human designing not to embody degrees of human interests, values, cognition, culture. Rather, this book attempts to "de-centre" the human, embracing anthropocentrism and the potential of human technologies to tune to aspects and forms of life that the dominant material culture makes difficult or impossible to attune to. This embracing of anthropocentrism is an effort to decouple from any (design) activity that would not acknowledge, through its practice, cohabitation with other beings, such as the extractivist and exploitative practices of the current capitalist-industrial complexes. It is also about nurturing an understanding of how we, as human beings, share in different degrees, the emergent properties of life in this planet. The approach will be to ground human signifying activities in shared semiotic activities with the rest of beings enacting the biosphere, the semiosphere, as will be discussed in the next chapter. As such, it is an approach to human designing as in an anthropology beyond the human, as Eduardo Kohn suggests, where human activities are understood as belonging to emergent dynamics, dynamics nested onto one another, from the abiotic to the biotic and increasing in complexity and semiotic freedom.[31]

Another aspect of the sentence "could I design a pot that would better accommodate a few of those creatures that I had already seen?" is the use of the first-person pronoun "I." In this attempt to think and do less anthropocentrically it is also difficult to say "I" and describe how "I" position myself as a designer in relation to the many "we" used in the book. There are several aspects worth keeping in mind from the outset. The "we" that I speak about sometimes refers to the general anthropocentrism that you as a reader share with me. For example, there are occasions when I use "we humans" to refer to this level of species-specific elements that characterize "us": being terrestrial creatures, warm-

---

[31] This entails an anthropology, which is the study of human societies and cultures and their development, that conceives human modes of being and knowing as sharing the same enactive principles with the rest of the living, departing from semiosis as a fundamental phenomenon of life. See Kohn (2013).

blooded, and so on. Yet, a great deal of effort in this book goes into recognizing diversity, diversity of human individuals, human cultures, societies, as well as diversity of species, species' individuals, species cultures, societies and their inter and intra-relations, basically the contingency and uniqueness of existence. Because of this, "us" never means a global all-encompassing "we" that homogenises, rather, an "us in all our differences through shared commonalities."

There is also something ineffable in using "I," something which relates strongly to the sense of poetics of this book. When saying "I," at work there is always an inhuman or ahuman dimension in and through us. Geologist Vladimir Vernadsky proclaimed a century ago that "we are walking talking minerals," that we are also "animated water,"[32] by now, at the second decade of the twenty first century we are aware that our sentience emerges not only from the mineral and chemicals flows to be found in the biosphere but also from complex bacterial ecologies that enact this multitudinous "I."[33] These are emergent and enactive processes that we share with all forms of life. Every time an "I" is written in these pages, it will tend to dissolve into that multiplicity. An "I" that resonates with the "I" of the opening quote of this Chapter, "I am therefore recounting my emotions when they encounter the emotions of other bodies and the emotions of the Biogea."[34]

Tuned to each other through evolution and adaptation, like the bee, we choose the flower, but the flower also chooses us, by attracting us with its shapes and colours. This is the "biological eroticism" of which Andreas Weber speaks of, we are webs of mutual transformation, always embodied. Weber writes, "biology is the erotic science *par excellence*, because a living being is an erotic process: It transforms itself through contact with others, imagining new relationships out of each existing one, desiring more life, unrelentingly seeking a connection to

---

[32] Vernadsky (1997 [1926]).

[33] See Gilbert and Epel (2015). Also Sagan (2011).

[34] Serres (2012: 118).

the whole of which it is both concentration and unrepeatable instantiation."[35]

The recognition of this continuum is fundamental in this book and sets the basis for the possibility to create a culture that shares and participates through its material flows in the collective becomings of all kinds of beings.

## AN APPROACH TO WRITING

As a reader you will notice that the passages, the sections of the book are separated by subtitles, and do not always follow one another in a completely linear narrative that builds up to the next section. Rather, the subtitles become hints for "dimensions" or "layers" that frame the issues discussed in particular ways. They present a series of "entries" onto issues explored diffractively, compositionally, iteratively, and partially. My hope is that these personal experiences will make sense, and that the beings and things presented in the coming pages become alive as the signs relate to you through this shared spatial temporality that we call writing.

[35] See Weber (2017: 33).

# 1   Poetics of Relating

That enchanting part of the marsh, with its forest of graceful
miniature trees, where the social trupials sang and wove their
nests and reared their young in company—that very spot is now, I
dare say, one immense field of corn, lucerne, or flax, and the
people who now live and labour there know nothing of its former
beautiful inhabitants, nor have they ever seen or even heard
of the purple-plumaged trupial, with its chestnut cap and its
delicate trilling song. And when I recall these vanished scenes,
those rushy and flowery meres, with their varied and multitudinous wild bird life—the cloud of shining wings, the
heart-enlivening wild cries, the joy unspeakable it was to me
in those early years—I am glad to think I shall never revisit
them, that I shall finish my life thousands of miles removed
from them, cherishing to the end in my heart the image of
a beauty which has vanished from earth.
*Far Away and Long Ago*, WILLIAM HENRY HUDSON

Humanity has lost winged eclipses.
But what the world has lost is not what people mourn.
What the world has lost, and what truly matters, is a part of what
invents and maintains it as world. The world dies from each
absence; the world bursts from absence. For the universe, as the
great and good philosophers have said, the entire universe feels and
thinks itself, and each being matters in the fabric of its sensations.
*It Is an Entire World That Has
Disappeared*, VINCIANE DESPRET

## DEVISING RESPONSES

Designing *devises*, which implies creating divisions, arranging partitions, material and sensible, including some and excluding others. At the same time, because design is a process of negotiation and mediation, it is connective and relational. Designed things work because they connect. Thus, a form of togetherness[1] is inscribed in, by and through things that tend to maintain us in our relating to (some) others. In this sense, there is a "gathering" performed by design. The norm of the devising through the dominant paradigm of design has been human; done by humans and for humans. If there is a togetherness with other species enacted through design, it is most clearly for humans and few other beings, those that we find edible, beautiful, useful, or "good" companions. Devising for some of "us," the privileged minority that consumes most, in the so-called Global North, whether this global north happens to be enacted in a geographic location that may or may not coincide with the geographical north of the equator of our planet.[2]

Designing results in the materialization of things that may, for example, constrain the influences and effects of the environment on us, as when a wall is built from mud to shelter us

[1] A more extended essay on "togetherness" was published as an entry in Staszowski and Tassinari (2020: 306–309).

[2] The term Global north functions in tandem with the term Global South, which "is employed in a post-national sense to address spaces and peoples negatively impacted by contemporary capitalist globalization. [. . . It] captures a deterritorialized geography of capitalism's externalities and means to account for subjugated peoples within the borders of wealthier countries, such that there are economic Souths in the geographic North and Norths in the geographic South. [. . .] the epithet 'global' is used to unhinge the South from a one-to-one relation to geography." See Mahler (2017). Global South and Global North are, like most concepts in my understanding, "shorthand" expressions to which we must remain attentive, as they risk perpetuating dichotomies that can become counterproductive to understand geopolitical and historical dynamics. A history of this expression and its relation to "design" (conceived as an imposition from the Global North) can be found in Alfredo Gutiérrez Borrero's doctoral thesis (Gutiérrez Borrero, 2021).

from the contingencies of weather. Design may also result in the materialization of things that may relieve us from making certain efforts, as when a cup is made in such a way and with such materials as to afford to contain liquids, so that we can easily drink from it. Design arranges partitions, these partitions include or enable relations with some-things, some-ones, and exclude or disable relations with some other-things, some other-ones. Devising is not an "either or" question; either we include, or we exclude, it is always "and." All devising creates inclusions *and* exclusions, intended *and* unintended. This is the seemingly paradoxical dimension of design, namely, that when we create, for example a car, we are creating the possibility of not only transporting ourselves from one place to another (i.e. relation to the effort of moving a body), but also the car crash (i.e. a relation between speed and encounters with unexpected bodies), or at another scale, global warming by means of the emissions of combustion engines (i.e. a relation with atmospheric gases); a thing and its "negative side", the accident. Parallel to every single invention design constantly creates the possibilities for new unexpected events. Design re-configures our environment by introducing new artefacts and triggers new demands of knowledge to every being and everything that comes in contact with the thing devised; hospitality and hostility are enacted through design on a daily basis.[3]

In the case of the pot for the plant where the pigeons are, it is not possible to say that the pigeons are excluded from this design, since the device affords their nesting. Rather, the exclusions happen in relation to most biological and ecological processes during production and of discard of the artefact (in the absence of recycling infrastructures in this area). Keeping in mind that the pot has been designed not for the whole of its lifecycle but only for a few instances of its cycle of use by a human user, it can be said that it has been conceived (formed/configured/materialised) for two basic functions: to hold a certain amount of soil that can provide enough nutrition to a small plant, and to allow

[3] Ávila (2012).

the drainage of water from the container of soil. The combination of these two functions makes it easy to transport and place in different contexts by a single person.

Yet, even when considering the so-called useful cycle of the pot, the "functions" are not only "functional" in the physical performativity of containing soil and draining water. Its design also "functions" as a *sign* to be interpreted by whoever may come across "the pot." Depending on who that is, these interpretations will vary, and a human acquainted with these artefacts may find this ceramic-like plastic piece appealing enough to use it to decorate a windowsill, while a bird that returns to the place where it was born may interpret it (in the absence of the trees or other material support that were there before) as affording an opportunity for nesting. A sign is "anything that indicates, shows the way, or makes evident something that would otherwise remain concealed or inaccessible" writes ecosemiotician Timo Maran.[4] In this sense and by reshaping entire landscapes, part of the hostility of devising things under an exclusively anthropocentric paradigm is that they break with the patterns that can be recognized as signs of affordances for the continuation of the rhythms and needs of other forms of life. What becomes explicit in this process is the degrees of violence enacted and inflicted upon all kind of beings by this devising, by this responding in general patterns that do not acknowledge the myriad beings that interpret the material signs that we produce.

When describing strategies of war literary critic Elaine Scarry writes "the goal of every strategic design is to actively withhold meaning from the opponent."[5] Although Scarry is referring to the verbal act of lying through, for example, codes that make meaning irrecoverable or difficult in order to divert an opponent in war situations, this short quote highlights the importance of making sense of environmental information. All living beings attune to certain patterns and regularities in the places where they live, but designing introduces, at a higher and higher pace,

[4] Maran (2020: 5).
[5] Scarry (1985: 133).

new things that create new patterns in environments without acknowledging other beings' capacities to adapt to them. Unwittingly, by excluding most other forms of sentience and perception, we have waged a not always silent war through the artefacts that mislead other-than-humans and afford them few possibilities for their self-realization.

## POETICS

Starting with Aristotle in ancient Greece, "poetics" has come to mean a systematic study of the enaction of works of art. Yet, any practice is poetic in a sense. The poet is a "maker," someone who creates, composes. The word comes from the Greek *poiētikos* which literally means "creative, productive" from *poiētos* "made" and *poiein* "to make." Making (poetics) is neither restricted to artistic practices, nor restricted to, or a privilege of, the human species, it is inherent to life. Poetics is also about expressiveness and meaning enacted and perceived through bodies, an emotional understanding that is a "shared existential experience—poetic objectivity" as Andreas Weber suggests.[6] For Weber,

> Poetic objectivity is not the objectivity of a scientist's proof. Scientific objectivity exercises imperial rule by excluding the subjectivity of living beings, which in truth is a crucial feature of the world. Poetic objectivity does not attempt to prevail. Poetic objectivity is deliberately weak. We cannot "prove" it with quantification or controlled, reproducible experiments. We can only try to bring it to the observer and let it do its work by transmitting the gift of life, by arousing the desire for aliveness. In this sense, poetic objectivity has more power than any scientific reasoning because we can feel it and because it can transform our actions even before our conscious minds can recognize it. Great literature is able

[6] Weber (2019: 139).

to transform a personal life, as is the experience of nature and the presence of other beings. Insights can be won not only by one's own experience, but also by experiencing crystallized poetic experience.[7]

The results of designing, the many artefacts that populate our everyday, are crystallizations of poetic experience, and as such have the potential to arouse the desire for aliveness. Yet, the relating through designing seldom encompasses other-than-humans in life-affirming ways, producing patterns that disconnect us from these life-enhancing possibilities. In the midst of so many absences of living creatures displaced by our designs, there is an urgent need to enact a culture that re-links to the living. As an approach, it has to cultivate "the art of paying attention," to paraphrase philosopher Isabelle Stengers, and the "arts of noticing" to say it with anthropologist Anna Lowenhaupt Tsing,[8] a process that must be actualized, constantly reinvented, if it is to remain attentive, if it is to become a "poetics of relating."

As such, the poetics of relating advocated here is based on poetic objectivity as "the ability to be touched," as Weber suggests, a human dialogic endeavour, a form of conversation across species that requires remaining vulnerable. It has less to do with trying to connect everything with everything else than about the act (and the art) of making connections; designing as an act of relating that attempts at relating with care while nurturing the *partial connections*[9] that may be shared.

The word poetic emphasizes the pleasurable engagement with things that are grasped yet not totally understood, something diffuse and agreeable that is composed, something akin to (the search for) beauty. A kind of perceptual seduction by actively partaking in affirming to some extent the life of some others.

---

[7] Weber (2019: 139–40). Weber's work is grounded on a poetic approach based on biosemiotic understandings. Other accounts of poetics from a biosemiotic perspective can be found in Wheeler (2016).

[8] See Stengers (2015: 62); and Tsing (2017: 17).

[9] A term coined by anthropologist Marylin Strathern. See the section "Partial connections" in Chapter 4.

Elaine Scarry writes: "It is not that beauty is life-threatening (though this attribute has sometimes been assigned it), but instead that it is life-affirming, life-giving; and therefore if, through your careless approach, you become cut off from it, you will feel its removal as a retraction of life."[10]

It is this retraction from life that W. H. Hudson perceives in the quote that opens the chapter and can be found in *Far Away and Long Ago. A Childhood in Argentina*, published in 1918. Hudson, convalescent in a hospital in London, recollected his childhood "in the Pampas." Those early days of illness at the hospital gave him a "wonderfully clear and continuous vision of the past," which motivated his recovery and urged him to recollect it and write it down in an autobiographical book. Although written more than hundred years ago, these paragraphs resonate intensively, perhaps more clearly now than then. The destructive patterns already perceptible at that time—the replacement of the variety of native species for the monocultures of "corn, lucerne, or flax"—continued to be perpetuated, thoroughly maintained, and further developed by capitalist-industrial complexes, throughout the twentieth century, which, in the early days of the second decade of the twenty-first century, still seems set on expanding.

In October 2015, I travelled to meet entomologist Mariano Lucia, with whom I was collaborating in the project "Spices-species," and visited him in La Plata, a city close to the region described by Hudson in the quote opening this chapter, south of what is today the city of Buenos Aires. During the short period I stayed in La Plata, I managed to visit Hudson's childhood house, in nearby Quilmes, which has become a museum and a small natural reserve. The visit was possible thanks to the generosity of the director of the museum, Rubén Ravera, who kindly drove me to the site and guided me on a day in which the place was closed. I was extra lucky that day, not only because of the kindness of Rubén, but also because we managed to visit the house at all, since local residents had that day organized "piquetes" or blockages of streets by burning tires protesting and claiming

[10] Scarry (1999: 27).

FIGURE 1.1  Children playing on streets with burning tyres in Quilmes. (Photo by author)

social justice. As we drove from La Plata to Quilmes, and just before taking the final turn that would lead to Hudson's childhood place, we met with the scene that you can see in Figure 1.1, of an everyday where children play and ride bikes around streets with burning tires, a violence normalised, a social reality with destructive social and ecological impact for the lives of everyone in the area, human and other-than-human.

If Hudson was correct, already in 1918, that the views of his childhood were gone and replaced by fields of corn, a century later, the fields in those very places have been replaced by provisional housing and poor infrastructure. The protests of people in the area often claim food, or a place in which to live, something relatively normal on the periphery of cities such as Buenos Aires. My literary encounters with Hudson's concerns for what we today call biodiversity loss was matched with the reality of those humans that cannot choose to take care of "the environment" since their reality is too oppressive. In spite of the locality (because of the locality), the childhood of those children will differ enormously from those who, like Hudson more than a hundred and fifty years ago, could afford food and recreation from the places where they were born.

The poetics of relating is therefore not necessarily always something "positive," something "constructive." The children in the image practice the relating to the possibilities afforded by their social and ecological environment. To say that designing for biological diversity is a poetics of relating exposes the intricacies and the risks of relating: To what? For whom? How? If "relation is the knowledge in motion of beings, which risks the being of the world" as Édouard Glissant suggests,[11] the risks call for poetic practices that enable care, practices that enable the perception of new registers for cohabitation, renewed aesthetic standards to perceive the hostility of the retraction of life.

## NATURALLY ARTIFICIAL

For humans it is natural to produce the artificial. However, what has been characteristic of most of what we call artificial, is that its results do not participate in life-affirming ways in the natural systems that enable them, nor in the life cycles of most other beings than humans. Yet, importantly, "life affirmation" cannot be considered "in general," "always," or "for all and all the time," a design project can only attempt to make differences to someone, somehow, somewhere, and these relations change in time. To exemplify how this approach could be realized through design, I will present some of my own projects (Chapter 2), which were situated and developed in the province of Córdoba, in the central region of Argentina. These projects, through design, trigger the explorations, speculations, and propositions of the book, aspects of the relationality of the natural–artificial continuum that may be called naturecultures, urban ecologies, agroecosystems, and other names, provided that these names indicate and help us to slow down to pay attention to the biotic–abiotic continuum, to the sensory materials that living beings encounter and inform behaviour.

---

[11] Glissant (1997: 187).

The projects are not projects that were designed *for* animals, or *for* plants, or any other-than-human *only*. The projects were designed *for humans with* other-than-humans and to account for local ecological realities. The projects are intended to displace unaware anthropocentrism; they do not claim to be non-anthropocentric but they do claim to be life-affirming. They need to be understood in their subtle but important differences with mundane artefacts such as a flowerpot, a shower grating, a door, a bench, or any other thing that exists in the everyday environments where we live. You may look around you if you are reading this book indoors and try to find something that has been designed with other-than-humans in mind. Take a moment to think about this. Is there anyone of the things that surround you, including the parts of the building you are in that has been conceived also to host more or other than human inhabitants?

I assume that you have not found any, and if any, certainly not many, very few things that form part of urban everyday life can be said to be intentionally inclusive of other forms of life. In this sense, the artefacts I present relate to but differ from, for example, "bee hotels," "bat houses," or bird feeders, to name a few of the most common ones we can find in cities. The artefacts presented in this book should be seen as part of the growing constellation of products for other-than-humans, but they need to be understood in their *questioning* of human everyday life, their social norms, and values.

What I am advocating for is an alternative design culture that tunes into localities and scaffolds the ecological realities of a place. If we understand scaffolding as a temporary structure for holding or supporting something, for example workers and materials while repairing or constructing a building, we can think of all kinds of structures that support all kinds of things: as such, words become devices that support cultural development,[12] tables become devices that support eating together in particular postures, and so on. In this sense, specific designs may materially scaffold a situation, as in the structure that holds the workers of a building, but there is another layer of scaffolding that is enacted by

[12] See Hoffmeyer (2008a: 138).

these things: *semiotic scaffolding,* which is not material but relational and enacted by complex webs of signification. Semiotic scaffolding is something that "canalizes further behaviour. It is the frame for habits . . . scaffolding is what results from learning" as described by biosemiotician Kalevi Kull,[13] therefore scaffoldings such as words or tables can, in their turn, scaffold further behaviour and afford refining conceptual models, or eating habits.

Scaffolding the ecological realities of a place as I wrote before, implies tuning into the needs and capacities of other creatures through material scaffoldings that can support their habits. This is crucial since the patterns to which they are habituated are disappearing due to human intervention. This tuning includes establishing dialogic relations with other creatures by attending to their signifying habits as they relate to the things we design. A designing that is response-able is adaptive and revises the signs that scaffoldings inscribe for those species involved, something to which we will return and discuss in more detail in Chapter 4.

It is not about supporting forms of life "in general" applying the same formulas everywhere, but specifically and in relation to the always different places that humans and others inhabit. We can consider beekeeping as an example. Of around 20,000 species of bees in the world, only seven to eleven species are recognized as honeybees, of which *Apis mellifera* is the best known. Beekeeping is characterised by the global maintenance of the population of *Apis mellifera,* a species native to Europe, the Middle East, and Northern Africa. In places other than these, let us say South America, and in spite of the commercial importance of this species (or particularly because of this), what would scaffold the ecological realities of the flowers and other species dependent on pollination in a given city, would be to create artefacts that relate specifically to bee species that are native or endemic to that region. The challenge is to relate to them in meaningful ways so that humans can value them for their difference and their participation in the enaction of the local ecology.

In this sense can an alternative artefact be partly conceived as an *alter-native,* as will be presented in Chapter 3. The notion

---

[13] Kull (2012: 227–230).

of *alter-native* demands making these distinctions and these relations explicit; to what extent can an artefact such as a beehive said to be "alter-native" when the materials that it is built from are from other parts of the world and the bees that are introduced and reproduce are alien to the ecosystems? In this questioning, the projects' intent is to engage, rather than control, to create design ecologies of care, by working through design in the becoming of these artefacts as we become otherwise through the affective ecologies we enact in relation to each other.

## MAINTAINING WORLDS

In the context of climate change induced by anthropogenic factors (which does not mean that all humans are equally responsible for these changes), this approach reconsiders relations to other species, considering biological diversity as a departure point to propose design. Climate change debates have been dominated by the metrics of economic and scientific disciplines. Most commonly, the type of information that leads these debates refers to the amount of carbon emissions to the atmosphere, that is, measurable, quantifiable data of some kind. Even though this information is concrete in its analytical specificity, it leads to abstraction in relation to the everyday life of most people,[14] only left with the hope that the newest technology (always in the future) will "solve" those issues. Designed artefacts can make a great difference as mediators of relations with environments and beings of all kinds. Maintaining biodiversity implies maintaining and adapting to worlds, the multiple experiential worlds of the species involved, human and other. We may react with fear, with curiosity, or with repulsion at encounters with beings we do not know, we dislike, or do not understand, in every case the emotional, perceptual, experiential, and embodied dimension of *a human world* is enacted. Design work that puts biodiversity as a starting dimension to engage with the pervasive lack of contact with plant and animal species, has to acknowledge the

[14] See Stoknes (2015).

affective ecologies that these imply. Qualities are as important as quantities. Metrics and conscious rationale cannot be dominant, but complementary to the qualitative and unconscious experiences of being alive. To engage through design in affirming local biological diversity, in our projects we have been not only seeking to understand how many species participate in certain forms of interaction, or how certain species may be able to travel specific distances in search for food or other quantitative aspects (see Figure 2.20 in Chapter 2), but also seeking the sensual and sensorial in-form-ation[15] that may affect, be valued, and incorporated to behavioural patterns. The reason, as in the example of the pot and the pigeons, is that design enacts the material and immaterial dimensions that afford all kinds of beings to be affected, and to engage in the possibilities of the physical and ecological realities they enact. Design prescribes ways of being and sensing, and thus mediates the possibilities of acting,[16] whether it is for a human or another being. The configurations that result from designing trigger (both by intention and accident) behaviour and in this sense, the loosening of control in a poetics of relating is about creating space for becoming with others in cohabitation, and attempting to understand the partitions, the divisions of devices, material and sensible.

## SIGNIFYING

By framing design through its meaning-making, its signifying dimension, the reasoning follows a basic (bio/eco)semiotic conception in which designing participates in the *semiosphere*. I have already been presenting semiotic concepts such as semiotic

---

[15] "The biological discipline morphology derives its name from the Greek word 'morph'. According to the etymological dictionary the romans probably took over this word from the Greek, but in a distorted way. Thus, In Latin 'morph' became 'form'. From this Latin word arose the verb *informare*: To bring something into form. And this again is the root of the now fashionable word *information*." See Hoffmeyer and Emmeche (1991).

[16] See Latour (1992).

scaffolding, and to better contextualize this and other notions to be further discussed, I would like to pay more attention to the phenomenon of semiosis. Semiotics is a field of study concerned with signs and signification, basically, the processes of meaning creation. Despite semiotics being the general science of signi-fication, historically, several strands of semiotics have mostly studied what today is understood as anthroposemiosis, and more particularly, the study of human communication and signification as an exceptional phenomenon based on human symbolic capab-ilities, something that separates humans from other beings. Today, the interdisciplinary fields known as biosemiotics and ecosemi-otics have expanded the human-centred approach and form a field that recognises that all life is grounded in semiotic processes.

Inscribing the (life) activities and results that we call design in this signifying continuum means recognizing that the differ-ences that designing makes are differences for all kind of beings, humans included. This implies considering that different species re-cognize things differently and thus that there is a need to incorporate interspecies *recognition* as a parameter in design to conceive and produce ideas.[17] If for humans it is natural to produce the artificial and what is called design does not engage in semiotic considerations of other-than-human modes of percep-tion, then the culture of the artificial can only become destructive of ecological relations.

What must be acknowledged is that designing is *necessarily* an entanglement of matter with semiosis. Even when the responses of design are conceived for humans only, designing is always enacting responses for a multiplicity of beings and systems that intra-act in relation to them. Paraphrasing Karen Barad,[18] we could say that design is a diffractive process, a meaning making

---

[17] Designing may follow contemporary environmental justice, which frames issues by distinguishing among distribution (who enjoys rights, responsib-ilities, costs), procedure (how decisions are made, who participates, on what terms), and recognition (respecting identities and cultural difference). See Martin, Coolsaet, Corbera, Dawson, Fraser, Lehman, and Rodriguez (2016: 254–261).

[18] Barad (2007: 89).

material discursive phenomenon, marking differences from within and as part of an entangled state with worlds and environments.

Designing is a dynamic response, part of a living process that engages in the devising of aliveness (or lack thereof) in the *semiosphere*, that is, in the enactment, production and circulation of signs. Biosemiotician Jesper Hoffmeyer redefined the semiosphere—a notion originally coined by Russian-Estonian semiotician Yuri Lotman—in this way, "[. . .] as a sphere like the atmosphere, hydrosphere, or the biosphere. It permeates these spheres from the innermost to outermost reaches and consists of communication: sound, scent, movement, colours, forms, electrical fields, various waves, chemical signals, touch and so forth—in short, the signs of life."[19]

Considering this definition, it is relevant to acknowledge that through the practice of design a wide range of "signs of life" have not been sufficiently valued, perceived, or allowed. Consequently, the signifying dimensions of the activity we call design are created bearing in mind, for the most part, human communication only. Yet it is important to remember that human communication and semiotic behaviour are not limited to natural languages such as English, Spanish, or Chinese. Non-symbolic signs, the ones that are indexical (based on physical or causal connections such as smoke coming from a chimney indicating the existence of fire) or iconic (based on similarity, such as the image of an animal on a road sign), are particularly important when thinking of design in relation to cognition and to action.[20] Design, as a human response, changes environments and enacts an ethical dimension by devising; each artefact connects and separates, and these inclusions and exclusions relate to the sensorial capacities of all species,

[19] Hoffmeyer (2008a: 5).

[20] The reader familiar with semiotic concepts will notice that this extremely simplified description follows a model of semiosis based on the category of sign as constituted by iconic, indexical, and symbolic dimensions; a model originally developed by philosopher and logician Charles Sanders Peirce. For an overview of how ecosemiotics adopts and complements with other modelling C. S. Peirce's semiotic model see Maran (2020). For a nuanced anthropological description of these signifying processes see Kohn (2013).

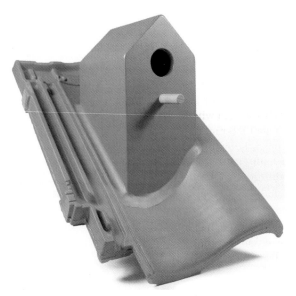

FIGURE 1.2  Birdhouse by Klaas Kuiken.
(Image courtesy of Klaas Kuiken)

producing "agential cuts," to describe it with the agential realism of Barad.[21]

If we pay attention to indexical and iconic aspects affecting behaviour across species, we can better understand design as a multispecies communicative phenomenon. For example, if on the roof of a house part of the tiling is made to resemble the shape of a human house, a human being would iconically associate the tile to a house and indexically connect it with the possibility for bird nesting (Figure 1.2).

The house-shaped "cavity" may not be perceived as a "house" by all kind of birds, but it may be recognized as a place affording nesting by some particular bird (and possibly other) species, and thus function as a "house." The notion of semiosphere helps

[21] Barad (2007: 148).

us be attentive to these processes of cognition. In the words of Hoffmeyer,

> The concept of semiosphere adds a semiotic dimension to the more well-known concept of the biosphere, emphasizing the need to see life as belonging to a shared universe of sign activity through which cells, organisms and species all over the planet interact in ways that we still hardly understand. Importantly, every single species (including humans) has only limited access to this semiosphere, because each species' capacity for sensing and interpreting potential cues in its surroundings, i.e. its interpretance, has evolved to fit a particular ecological niche. Put in the terminology of Jacob von Uexküll, each species is confined to its own limited Umwelt, or "internal model" with which individual of a species constructs an understanding of its surroundings.[22]

Although technology extends (but also limits) our human Umwelt, responding through designing has generally implied the reinforcement and development of the dominant culture that interferes with the lifecycles of most species across almost every scale from the local to the global. This does not suggest that what we call the artificial does not support at all the proliferation of any form of life; there have always been species that have benefited from and adapted to human forms of habitation, whether humans planned for that or not, as we will see in the coming chapter when discussing not only domestic or wild animals, but also liminal species, which are those that are in-between these two common animal imaginaries and form part of the majority of beings of the planet. If designing is to participate in life-affirming ways in the lifecycles of other than human species, then the understanding of multispecies meaning making is fundamental as it engages humans in affective ecologies. Andreas Weber writes: "Nature is basically meaning centred, open to creative change, bringing forth agents with subjective experiences and always

---

[22] Hoffmeyer (2008b: 149–166).

creative in realizing the individual through the whole. It generates feelings to accompany any exchange-relationship, which is
always both metabolism and meaning."[23]

If we are not affectively involved in the maintenance and
becoming of the relations to these beings in the places we inhabit,
the meaning created through designing becomes sterile or destructive to other-than-humans and thus impoverishes ecological
relations making ecosystems more vulnerable. Conversely, this
suggests how designing could, paraphrasing Weber, intensify
experiential and expressive depth. In this context, designing
becomes (de)signing (Chapter 4), that is, a human activity that
acknowledges its own meaning-making processes while attentive to other beings' capacities to interact with the signs enacted
through the artificial. In this way, more-than-human needs and
expressions may start to be recognized, valued and become
inscribed in the knowledge and practice of design. Yet, the challenges are not only to tune into and participate in the
complexity of ecological relations, but while doing so, of addressing "agents with subjective experiences" as Weber puts it. Since
"agents" refer to not only human but also other-than-human actors,
this, without a doubt, requires a transdisciplinary challenge with
an amplitude that we have simply not witnessed yet in a massive
scale, but that is starting to emerge across different fields by
scholars and practitioners of different kinds who, in their own
ways and through their practices, attempt at composing with
care, at remaining attentive to the cultural, historical, geopolitical and ecological issues in non-dualistic ways.

## THROUGH DESIGN

The importance of design-driven explorations lies in the need
to materialize naturecultures that engage us in living processes
and affect us materially, sensually, and on an everyday basis.

[23] Weber (2019: 169). As with the concept of intra-action, these relational and
non-dualistic approaches indicate that what we deem "real" is a contingent
network of dependencies. See also Sharma (2015).

Things that confront us with other modes and other possibilities of engagement and trigger alternative responses through their presence. Research through-design was the means of inquiry to develop the projects that I will be presenting in the next chapter. The projects are "essayistic," in the sense that they are attempts at thinking through materials and processes, probing thoughts, and becoming expressions of thinking.

Continuing with the signifying aspect of design, design knowledge often manifests itself as other-than-verbal knowledge (visual, tactile, auditive), and the differences inscribed by design inform behaviour for all kind of species, whether we who have made those designs have been aware of it or not. Explorations through-design are needed to complement the rationale and the type of logical implications of inquiries based on natural languages. In this sense, the design-driven explorations intend to expand *aísthesis*, sense perception, and work in tension with the *anaes-thesia* that may occur by distancing ourselves from the situations if only engaging, in abstraction, with ideas through natural languages.

The design propositions of the three projects in the coming chapter were elaborated through the constraints of the ecological realities of each of the specific contexts. They were not abstract responses that could be implemented without consideration of locality but particular responses to specific local situations. As such, a certain type of design knowledge and understanding is produced in constant negotiation with the specifically situated knowledge and constraints of the project and differs thus from explorations and propositions that are mostly linguistic in character and tend towards detachment from locations by appealing to the human symbolic order (nominalist-conceptual, linguistic conventions)[24]. As mentioned, design inscribes and prescribes not only symbolic knowledge, but also iconic and indexical knowledge that affords interpretation by other-than-human beings.

[24] Speaking specifically about plants, philosopher Michael Marder comments "The aesthetic attitude, broadly conceived, seems to be more propitious to a nonviolent approach to plants than either their practical instrumentaliz-ation or their nominalist-conceptual integration into systems of thought." See Marder (2013: 4).

Design, to different extents, has always dealt with control.
The case studies of the book are examples of the negotiations
and compromises between controlling and the letting go of control
to accept and embrace other modes of being. A delicate compositional process that requires attentiveness to the many voices
and to the many beings with which we cohabit, regardless of the
environment where we may be. This compositional process is
what may lead to a poetics of relating which may enable "ecologies of practices" that trigger design ecologies which in turn
reinforce ecologies of practice.[25]

With this background, "through-design" means not only the
practice of designing, as in visualizing, modelling, or prototyping
which, in their multisensorial spectra, engages in other forms of
knowing than the linguistic, but also and crucially, the engagement "through-design" *in* and *with* the particular more-than-human
ecologies, ethologies, by which we become affected as we relate
to the beings studied and to their specific geopolitical histories
and habitats.

## ECOLOGIES

Throughout this book, ecologies of practice will be understood
and framed by combining psychological, social, and environmental levels, building on the work of psychiatrist and philosopher

[25] In "Introductory notes on an ecology of practices" Isabelle Stengers writes:
"An ecology of practices may be an instance of what Gilles Deleuze called
'thinking par le milieu', using the French double meaning of milieu, both
the middle and the surroundings or habitat. 'Through the middle' would
mean without grounding definitions or an ideal horizon. 'With the surroundings' would mean that no theory gives you the power to disentangle
something from its particular surroundings, that is, to go beyond the particular towards something we would be able to recognise and grasp in spite
of particular appearances. Here it becomes clear why ecology must always
be etho-ecology, why there can be no relevant ecology without a correlate
ethology, and why there is no ethology independent of a particular ecology.
[. . .] In the same way, I would venture there is no identity of a practice
independent of its environment." Stengers (2005).

Félix Guattari. Guattari outlined and discussed the overlaps of
these "ecologies" in his book *The Three Ecologies*. In that book
Guattari sketches an ethico-political articulation that he called
an *ecosophy*, based on three ecological registers: a mental ecology,
a social ecology, and an environmental ecology, all simultan-
eously present and mutually influencing, "overlapping," or
"intersecting." Guattari's insight was not only the intersectional
aspect—the understanding that from the overlap, from the conflu-
ence, of more than one section emerges something "greater"
than the "parts"[26]—but also the explicit articulation of the psychological dimension as generative (desire-production) and
inextricably related to the social and environmental dimensions.
For Guattari, to explicitly address the psychological register was
a way to critically engage with production-consumption cycles
of what he called "Integrated World Capitalism", which in his
words, "[. . .] tends increasingly to decentre its sites of power,
moving away from structures producing goods and services
towards structures producing signs, syntax and—in particular,
through the control which it exercises over the media, advert-
ising, opinion polls, etc.—subjectivity."[27]

Through this framing, the human subject becomes prominent in its capacity to engage not only with and through
environmental and social ecologies, but also with and through
ecologies of ideas and sensibilities enacted by signification. As
a conceptual model, the three ecologies help us to appreciate
the potential combination of signs and encounters, internal and
external (intra-active) to any human being. The acknowledgement of this complexity requires the re-cognition and appreciation
of intra-activity, and the re-cognition and appreciation of others'
differences and capabilities. Crucial to this, as mentioned previously, is an understanding of the category of "species" in its
dynamism, relationality, and fluidity. The word is a shorthand
that acknowledges that "species" is based on family resemblances

[26] This common expression should be understood as shorthand, yet we should
    notice that things are not parts in interaction, but things mutually consti-
    tuted. See Sharma (2015).
[27] Guattari (2008 [1989]: 32).

and is a category that is fundamentally fuzzy, there is only differential becoming, multiplicity, and specificity.[28] This triple overlapping register could also be used to frame studies and speculations upon other-than-human capacities and ways of being, to explore their differential becoming, multiplicity, and specificity. Can we speak of psychological, social, and environmental ecologies of all living beings? Even though what is understood as psychological in human beings differs from the processes of individuation of plants, all living beings establish degrees of social and environmental relations.[29] If we follow what Guattari means by subjectivity, it is important to understand that for him subjectivity is, at the same time, both collective and auto-producing. Auto-producing, in reference to biologists Humberto Maturana and Francisco Varela's notion of *autopoiesis* (the metabolic, self-maintaining chemistry of living cells)[30] and collective in its *sympoiesis*, through emphasis on the relational, historical, and situatedness of the collective becoming of subjectivity. This (transversalist) approach to subjectivity eludes the individual–social distinction as well as the conception of the subject either as a person or individual. Through this definition the boundaries psychological–social get even more diffuse and have to be considered in their mutually constitutive psychological–social–environmental dimensions.

Barad mentions that conceived intra-actively, beings, as phenomena, "exist only as a result of, and as part of, the world's ongoing intra-activity, its dynamic and contingent differentiation into specific relationalities . . . All real living is meeting. And each meeting matters."[31] In this living where each meeting matters, the mattering that we do through design imposes meaning. This meaning, to be of ecological relevance, must also make sense to other-than-human beings. How can we conceive artefacts, in their alterity, in their otherness, in such a way that they engage in the life and death of the species and the ecosystems where

[28] See Hendlin (2016: 94–110).

[29] See Marder (2013). Also, Despret (2016).

[30] See Maturana and Varela (1980). Also, Maturana and Varela (1998).

[31] Barad (2007: 353).

they may be used, produced, and discarded? I will return to these questions in Chapter 3, using the notion of *alter-natives* and through design examples.

## PROBING

The work presented here is "essayistic," not only because in my own projects "through-design" I attempt to think through material configurations and processes, probing thoughts and becoming expressions of thinking, but also because the probing and the thinking that these works do attempt to re-imagine ways of relating that, in their tensions and dynamics, draw upon different kind of knowledges, different kind of experiences, and different kind of perceptual capacities.

I believe that design can inform and co-create knowledge about ecologies as much as science does. Both design and science have contributed to ecological knowledge as well as the devastation of the environment, like design, science has been complicit in developing destructive industries, destructive cultures. This is one of the reasons why we should not conceive design in only positive terms ("solutions oriented," "constructive" . . .), but also to embrace the risks of bringing something new, the potential of any device, both its hospitality *and* its hostility.

Anthropologist Gregory Bateson has written that "Science *probes*; it does not prove," he was referring to the concern that,

> Not only can we not predict into the next instant of the future, but, more profoundly, we cannot predict into the next dimension of the microscopic, the astronomically distant, or the geologically ancient. As a method of perception—and that is all science can claim to be—science, like all other methods of perception, is limited in its ability to collect the outward and visible signs of whatever may be truth. Science *probes*; it does not prove.[32]

---

[32] Bateson (2002 [1979]: 27).

The complementarity to science's probing of nature is designing's probing of human everyday life, which lies in the qualitative, sensual, affective dimension that engages in specific patterns of living. By redesigning things that may contribute to a probing that *diverges*[33] from existing patterns and affirms the living by engaging in its divergent ways, and via these divergent knowledges "cause those who gather around it to think and hesitate together."[34] Designing explores possibilities of human life and of how humans can relate to what is not human. Through this probing, it may become more ecologically realistic to probe co-adaptive capabilities and explore the signs that can contribute to a healthier semiosphere. What we know is that, so far, the gatherings of design are far too partial for enabling long-term cohabitation.

This book is about probing, seeking, exploring connections, articulating design ecologies that enact ecologies of practice, of sensing, of being, which may help to conceive less partial, more inclusive devices. The urgency of mass extinctions and the threat that that implies for humans and all other species in all parts of the world demands immediate responses from all kind of prac-

[33] Isabelle Stengers develops the notion of *divergence* based on the work of Gilles Deleuze and Félix Guattari. For Stengers, divergence is "that which makes an aspect of this world matter" (2015: 144). "[. . .] the manner in which a practice, a way of life, or a being diverges designates what matters to them, and this is not in a subjective but a constitutive sense" (2015: 112). Deleuze wrote (*The Logic of Sense*) that only diverging lines communicate (saying that communication is creation, not redundancy). But diverging is not "from something." It designates what matters for you, and how it matters (in the positive sense), and therefore allows for symbiotic alliances, always lateral, never grounded on a "same" that would transcend or reconcile them. See https://quod.lib.umich.edu/o/ohp/12527215.0001.001/1:19/--architecture-in-the-anthropocene-encounters-among-design?rgn=div1;view=fulltext. Accessed June 21, 2021.

[34] Stengers (2015: 143). Stengers adds "It should be unnecessary to emphasize that making divergences present and important has nothing to do with differences of opinion, it must be said. It is the situation that, via the divergent knowledges it activates, gains the power to cause those who gather around it to think and hesitate together. I would go so far as to say that the achievement of an alloying, of a practice of the heterogeneous, doesn't require a respect for differences but an honouring of divergences." (2015: 143).

tices, to become able to shift to an ecological paradigm and in the case of this book, through the practice of design. Vincianne Despret writes that "What the world has lost, and what truly matters, is a part of what invents and maintains it as world. The world dies from each absence; the world bursts from absence."[35] We cannot perpetuate the inertia of the current paradigm with its anthropocentric and colonial patterns. Paraphrasing Despret one could say that each being matters and each artefact that we bring to the world "matters in the fabric of its sensations." Some worlds are materialized over others, and the inclusions and exclusions of each devising matters, and matters differently.

In the following chapter we will consider the probing enabled through some collaborative projects that I have developed, presented here as some responses that attempt to compose with others and to sketch a practical etho-ecological ethics[36] as poetics of relating.

[35] See Despret in Rose, van Dooren, and Churley (2017: 219–220).
[36] See Hendlin (2019).

# 2   Responding

Symbiogenesis is far more splendid than sex as a generator
of evolutionary novelty.
*Symbiotic Planet*, LYNN MARGULIS

The goal is to foster more hospitable contexts for human sense-
making so that humans can become productive participants in
the nourishing cycles of the biosphere, and not be mere bystand-
ers or exploiters of it (i.e., producers and consumers). Being an
active participant in the biosphere does not mean obeying all its
laws, but enacting freedom within the constraints of existential
and ecological necessity.
*Enlivenment*, ANDREAS WEBER

## RESPONSE-ABILITY

"To promise in return," this is what the word "response" means
if one follows its Latin origin, from the word *respondēre*. "Response"
is also related to another Latin word, *sponsor*, which means
guarantor. Elaborating on these, one could say that as a form of
human response, design (for the most part) has unknowingly
"promised in return" transformations for the benefit of
some members of some human groups, at least in the short term.
In most cases, what human systems "return" happens without
sufficient ecological knowledge or care; matter is inevitably
redistributed, but the misplacing of the chemicals that
constitute most of our material culture docs not contribute

to the diverse lifecycles of the beings that live where the materials happen to be extracted from and discarded onto. Biotic and abiotic systems, however, have attuned to one another through co-evolution and adaptation where responses are complemented. In short, what our behaviour (through collective industrious activities) sponsors, is a "return" of chemicals that do not belong to the ecosystems where they will be placed, as well as a "promise" of continuing to interrupt the lifecycles of most other beings.

As an ability to respond, design has proven to contribute to a disentanglement from the web of life, by engaging "us" in patterns that mostly support the short-term life-style of some humans. Acknowledging this, how could a design practice be reconceived to reimagine human and other-than-human abilities to mutually respond in life-affirming ways? What other expressions would a less anthropocentric design practice generate by becoming attentive to the perceptual capacities and needs of other species? The work that is necessary for us to undertake today is about fostering the human ability and capacity to respond in enlivening ways, by means of tuning human artifice to relate constructively to other-than-human beings, "enacting freedom within the constraints of existential and ecological necessity" as Weber puts it.[1] In this sense, it is less about the ability or the capacity to respond than it is about the way to respond (design is about "hows"): designing as an art of responding. An act of responding that acknowledges ecological constraints and which in its accountability becomes able to respond in life-affirming ways, becoming response-able, as Donna Haraway would have it.

Designing plays a role in creating registers to acknowledge and change how the world "is" and how it "works," and therefore, what it may become. Design can therefore participate in creating affective ecologies whereby we (and here "we" refers to humans and other-than-humans together) can establish contact with one another, directly or indirectly. We can be rendered sensible, we can practice attunement, to other living forms in concrete ways through how we, humans, design.

[1] Weber (2019: 130).

Here I am not proposing that designed artefacts should replace things such as trees for things such as pots specially designed for birds or any other being that participates in the life of the tree, quite the opposite. As mentioned earlier designed responses should *complement* conservation work to increase biodiversity. Through designing for interdependence we can explore how we become part of the worlds of others, and how they become part of our worlds, while keeping in mind that these *worlds*[2] are ontologically not identical; worlds are "brought forth" by living beings in all their variety. In this sense, a "world" differs from an "environment," in the words of biologist Francisco Varela,

> On the one hand, a body interacts with its environment in a straight-forward way. These interactions are of the nature of macrophysical encounters–sensory transduction, mechanical performance, and so on–nothing surprising about them. However, this coupling is possible only if the encounters are embraced from the perspective of the system itself. This embrace requires the elaboration of a surplus signification based on this perspective; it is the origin of the cognitive agent's world. Whatever is encountered in the environment must be valued or not and interacted with or not. This basic assessment of surplus signification cannot be divorced from the way in which the coupling event encounters a functioning perceptuo-motor unit.[3]

To be exposed to and by attending to, differences in worlds, design materializations offer a particular possibility by probing speculatively alternative ways of relating. As a practice that

[2] The word "world" will be used throughout this book as synonymous with "Umwelt," as conceived by biologist Jacob von Uexküll and further developed within biosemiotics. Uexküll's notion of Umwelt designates a sphere of the senses, a perceptual world in which an organism exists and acts, and thus, indicates the partiality of every species' perceptions and constitution of their world. See Von Uexküll (2001, 2010) and Hoffmeyer (2008a).

[3] Varela (1999: 55–56).

devises, that inscribes material and immaterial arrangements that form "partitions" which can be sensed and felt, these partitions should be understood in explicit political terms as "partitions of the sensible."[4] In this way design can support an explorative practice to articulate ecological and political aspects of our delegation of agency to artefacts. Acknowledging differences in response-abilities across species opens up for the possibility to conceive artefacts that engage local actors in particular socio-ecological dynamics. A worlding which implies that responses are concrete, not abstract, in the sense that they do not originate from a design conception where an artefact could be used in *any* environment but from a conception of artefacts created for specific places, for specific worlds.

The dominant global capitalist–industrial complex has accustomed us to artefacts that are designed in one location (using digital tools) to produce these artefacts in other locations, all without socio-ecological insight into the many localities where things will be used. Lamps, chairs, telephones, kettles, and most of what populates an average home in any city have been designed in places such as Milan, to be manufactured in places such as Shenzhen, to be used (and discarded) in places such as Guayaquil. Yet, the designers' (manufacturers, producers, etc.) intentions have been that these artefacts participate in a very basic sense in the life of a few of those who live in cities such as Guayaquil. The artefacts perform simple functions, in the case of a chair, of support, the affordance to sit on, and thus of benefit for a human regardless of where this person happens to live. This is the type of abstraction produced by designing. But it does not acknowledge location—meaning "not simply a physical point or place, but a historical–geographical epistemological location, a place that has been shaped by wider social, cultural, and economic processes that have shaped certain ways to make sense of the world."[5] A

[4] I am borrowing this term from Rancière (2010) A more thorough elaboration of this political aesthetics in relation to other-than-humans can be found in Ávila and Ernstson (2019). See also Chapter 4.

[5] Ernstson and Sörlin (2019: 22). This relates to Val Plumwood's notion of "shadow places" as will be developed in Chapter 3.

location or a place with specific ecological circumstances which affect all those living there, humans and others. Thus, the concrete worlding required to counter this designing that produces abstraction from and in locations, is a worlding which does not create a local–global dichotomy but is rather a grounding of responses that are partial, limited, and meant to participate in the lives of those living in those regions.

## ABOUT THREE PROJECTS

In the following pages I will be presenting three projects which are design-driven inquiries that I initiated and pursued together with different collaborators, all of them co-designed with Leonardo López. The projects probe and speculate upon the use of certain artefacts in everyday situations to make explicit some of their ecological implications. They are efforts to confront us with alternative yet possible realities, in which human users of these artefacts would engage in the caring of other-than-human beings in different ways. I write "would engage" because the projects were never intended to be "implemented," produced in series to be commercially or otherwise available for use. In this book these three projects work as case studies to elaborate upon, as I discuss them together with other projects to be introduced in Chapter 3.

The projects were developed in Argentina in the contexts of different phases of research,[6] yet at stake in all of them is establishing contact with at least one animal or plant species, in a way that engages us in their lives in one way or another and

[6] The mutualistic radio was one of the artefacts of a project entitled "¡Pestes!" (2011), part of my doctoral studies (Ávila, 2012). "Spices-species" and "Doomestics" were part of postdoctoral work entitled "Symbiotic tactics", (financed by the Swedish Research Council, 2013–2016). Besides the collaboration with Leonardo López, we were consulting a variety of experts, in the case of the postdoctoral work, most of them related to the Multidisciplinary Institute of Vegetal Biology (IMBIV), through the guidance of Gabriel Bernardello.

expands ecological understanding of the places for those that inhabit these locations. None of them are "solutions" to "problems," rather, they are responses to challenge dominant views and expectations while presenting alternatives that were technologically viable at the time they were conceived.

## Mutualistic radio

All artefacts affect ecologies, yet we have simply paid little or no attention to how artificial compositions may establish relations with living beings. Could artefacts engage in forms of symbiosis with specific biotic or abiotic systems? "¡Pestes!" was the working title of a project that addressed this question.

In this project I worked with radios, and I had chosen the radio as a generic "artefact" that represents so-called consumer products. Part of the criteria for choosing the radio was the need to work with the design of an artefact that could be mobile, that would be "simple" yet have a range of material and immaterial aspects (in our choice, the materiality of the component parts, the "immateriality" of radio waves) and an artefact that would be familiar to most people. The proposal does not suggest a "better" radio (it is actually very impractical) but is a suggestion of a possibility to engage with another being in a mutually beneficial way. The background to my inquiries at the time was the theme of hospitality and hostility. And by pursuing the quest to understand host–guest relations from different perspectives, I started to work with the category of symbiosis, used in biology to classify host–guest relations in three ways: *parasitism*, that is, a relation where one of the organisms benefits while the other one is harmed by the relation; *commensalism*, that is, a relation where one of the organisms benefit while the other one is indifferent to the relation; and *mutualism*, a relation where both organisms benefit from the relation. These three categories are dynamic (nothing is ever static!), and thus, forms of relation that may start as parasitism can lead to commensalistic or even mutualistic relations with time, as is the case with bacterial relations that may have started as parasitical but which have co-evolved and become incorporated through symbiogenesis, enacting the digestive or immune systems of all kinds of species.[7]

I proposed three radios[8] and each radio was designed considering a specific "ecological niche," a location, attending to some particular biophysical constraints. In these locations, each radio corresponded to a symbiotic category which led to three proposals: a parasitic radio, a commensalistic radio, and a mutualistic radio. I will briefly introduce this last one, a radio by which a human and another living being benefit from the relation with the artefact.

The proposal was situated in a region called La Calera, in an area with a small river. Studying different possibilities to engage with local actors, we decided to propose a radio that runs on electric energy generated by the pressure from the movements of water flow in conjunction with the energy provided by the biting (on the terminal made of balanced food) of *Serrasalmus spilopleura*, a local fish called "palometa" (Figures 2.1a and 2.1b). The piezo-electric devices designed to oscillate with the water flow as well as the biting obtain and transmit the 3V necessary to run the device (Figures 2.2, 2.3 and 2.4). As such, the mutualism proposed here is about the relationship with the fish, where the providing of food in exchange for energy is seen as mutually beneficial.

We can see in Figures 2.1a and 2.1b images of two specimens of *Serrasalmus spilopleura*, one of them being affected by a parasitical fungus, common in this species at that time. This led to a speculation about the possibility of redesigning the food on the piezo-electric terminals (Figure 2.3) to include medicinal ingredients to help the fish restore their health. In this way, we could increase the level of mutualism with this species, which could have higher/lower degrees of benefit. Here we were confronted with a choice, suggesting balanced food with medicinal properties made explicit an anthropocentric bias: our capacity to empathise with the fish. Without fully understanding their

---

[7] See Sagan (2011).

[8] See Ávila (2012), also https://www.martinavila.com/projects/pestes/

FIGURE 2.1 Two fish of the species *Serrasalmus spilopleura*. The bottom image is of an individual affected by fungi. (Photos by author)

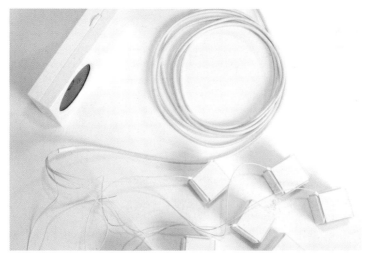

FIGURE 2.2  Radio, cables, and piezo-electric terminals. (Photo by Diego Combina)

FIGURE 2.3  Detail of pyramidal shapes of the balanced food that conform the piezo-electric terminals. (Photo by author)

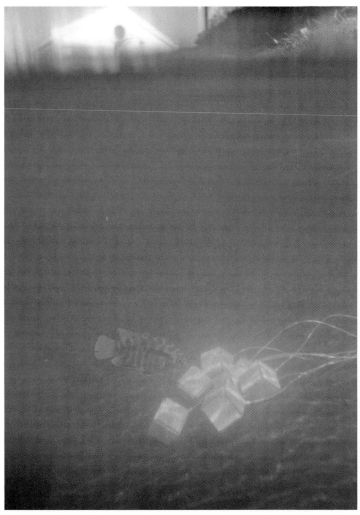

FIGURE 2.4 Fish (*Serrasalmus spilopleura*) biting piezo-electric terminals. (Photomontage based on photograph by Diego Combina)

ecological roles, intuitively, we were preferring the fish rather than the fungi. It would also be possible to devise an alternative that stimulates the advance of fungi, provided that we sympathised, if not directly with the fungi, at least with the idea of a mutually beneficial relationship at some other ecological scale.

Affective ecologies are always at work and precede designing. The practice of design has always been ethico-aesthetic[9], a *poethics*[10], and our bodies play a role, making poetics species specific. Philosopher Judith Butler mentions,

> it seems that the ways that others act upon us, without our will, constitutes the occasion of an ethical appeal or solicitation. This means that we are acted on, and solicited, ethically, prior to any clear sense of choice. To be impinged upon by another assumes a bodily proximity, and if it is the "face" that acts upon us, then we are to some extent affected and claimed by that "face" at the same time. On the other hand, our ethical obligations extend to those who are not proximate in any physical sense, and do not have to be part of a recognizable community to which we both belong. Indeed, for Levinas, those who act upon us are clearly other to us; it is precisely not by virtue of their sameness that we are bound to them.[11]

Even if we understood "face" in non-literal terms, the faces of fish have a stronger resonance in most of us than those of fungi, not only because of morphological correspondences such as eyes, mouth, and so on, but because of proximity of the scale of our bodies. The fungi, as entities to be considered in ethico-ecological terms are likely to be dismissed prior to any form of understanding of their ecological role in a given environment.

[9] See Guattari (1995) [1992]. Also Varela, F. (1999); Kriti Sharma's contingent account of ethics in Sharma, K. (2015); and Yogi Hendlin's account of biosemiotic ethics in Hendlin (2019).
[10] Borrowing the term from Anna Maria Orrù in a slightly different manner. See Orrù (2017).
[11] Butler (2011: 6).

By conceiving the radio in relation to specific beings in a particular ecological niche, the focus of the design becomes displaced from their traditional human-centredness to the possibility of participating in the life of others, at stake, however, is always the decision, conscious or not, of choosing *which others*.

One lesson learned from this project was that each location became a source of discovery and potential for becoming co-enacted in relation to a device, each actor investigated, examined for its capacities, abilities, not to use them but to engage in a co-adaptive possibility. Historically, unexpected events have led to aleatory combinations, pushing systems and organisms to cohabit in whatever circumstances, and to the testing of resilient capabilities and their life in symbioses. Framed by Lynn Margulis' phrase "symbiogenesis is far more splendid than sex as a generator of evolutionary novelty,"[12] our radio is a response that probes the possibility for cohabitation, for co-adaptation. And new challenges arise from this hypothetical relation, to name a few: how often would a person be there to match the predictability or unpredictability of the availability of food for fish that live in that location? How dependent may the fish become on the food which is external to their habitats? Could the radio become an instrument to engage in the life of the fish, so that it becomes a trigger to the maintenance of the relations?

We speculated upon cooperation rather than competition to become the drive of co-adaptation and co-evolution. I believe that the potential for enlivening, by looking at locations as sources of possibilities in combination with the ambition to support the lives of some of those that we could relate to consciously can be an inspiring paradigm to work with design and biodiversity. This life-affirming attitude is far from the negative approach of the reduce-reuse-recycle as generative logics for design,[13] yet it

[12] Margulis writes "Sex differs from symbiosis in that the cyclical fusion and later separation tend to be far more predictable, far less creative and casual than those in temporary symbiosis. In sex, offspring greatly resemble their parents, and gender differences are ritualized and predictable." (Margulis, 1998: 89).

[13] Relating to so-called "Eco-Positive Design" See the entry for Eco-positive design in Kothari, Salleh, Escobar, Demaria, and Acosta (2018).

should follow cyclic and thermodynamic principles. Because of this, and importantly, the naming of this artefact as "mutualistic," could only be reasonable if we only paid attention to the useful cycle, during the period when a human user is using it to listen to radio, rather than the whole of the life cycle of the radio (Fig. 2.5). The radio establishes relations through its processes and components, throughout the whole of its lifecycle, from production to discard. Ideally, each of these components will participate in the local social and environmental ecologies from cradle to cradle, where the materials may become food for others or part of an industrial metabolism.

## Spices-species

I have in mind a phrase that Gilles Deleuze and Félix Guattari once wrote: "drunkenness as a triumphant irruption of the plant in us."[14] In a sense, this is what this project was about, everyday life at an "intimate" scale; based on the relations we humans establish with plants by ingesting them, either because they are edible or because they can be used for medicinal purposes. Plants affect us, they inter- and intra-act through their chemistry and materiality with our bodies, they appeal to humans and many others by attracting us through the beauty of their flowers, the colour of their fruits, the shape of their blades, trunks, leaves. They irrupt in us in myriad ways, triumphantly or not they can cure and can kill, feed, and poison.

Plants, like any other living being, cannot be considered in isolation, without taking into account their pollinators, soils, light, and others. With this in mind, the wordplay of the working title "Spices-species" framed our ambition to design something that will make us not only relate to the plants that people in this region use, but also to relate to species that are important to the plant, at least, their main pollinators.

After discussions with biologists working with plants in different contexts, one of the aspects that framed the project

[14] Deleuze and Guattari (2004 [1980]: 12)

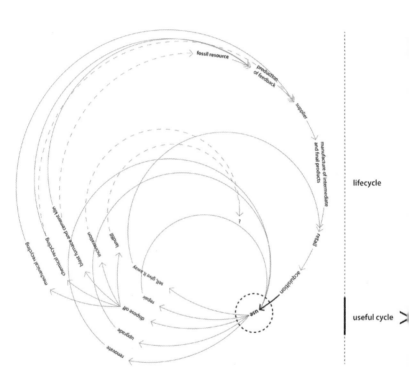

FIGURE 2.5 Lifecycles are not only useful cycles. (Illustration by author)

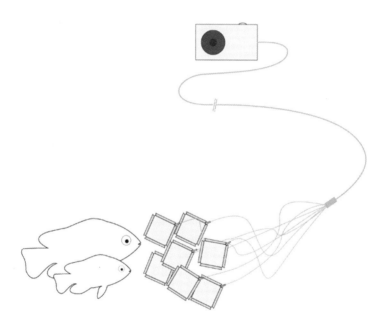

was the decision to work with plants that produce flowers, under-standing that in the urban context we were studying there was a general human predilection for floral plants, with the resulting presence or absence of certain plant species in the city of Córdoba. Together with researchers from the Multidisciplinary Institute of Vegetal Biology, we identified four floral native species of this region that could be either edible, medicinal, or both. These were: *Tagetes minuta*, *Caesalpinia gilliiesi*, *Nicotiana glauca* and *Passiflora caerulea*. After an initial year of studying, growing, and experimenting with the four of them, we decided to develop our proposal based on *Passiflora caerulea*, a variety of passion-flower, for being both medicinal and edible, and for specific interactions they have with carpenter bees that make them vulner-able in the built environment of the city of Córdoba.

Varieties of passionflower grow in different locations. In the central regions of Argentina, the variety known as *Passiflora caerulea* is mostly used for ornamental purposes, while its fruits are eaten and its parts (leaves, flowers, stems, and fruits) are used to make infusions and tinctures that alleviate humans with its sedative and anti-stress effects which one of the reasons why it is, perhaps, the most cherished of the native medicinal plants in the region. Several other species have a preference for this plant: *Agraulis vanillae maculosa*, called "espejitos" in the region, is the most common Argentinean butterfly and lays eggs and feeds on it, several carpenter bees of the genus *Xylocopa* prefer it for its abundant nectar, a variety of birds feed on its fruits, and ant species cohabit peacefully with some of its visitors to draw mutually beneficial relations that maximize the availability of nectar. These are a few of the most common interactions that are visible to the human eye, which give a sense of their co-evolutionary symbiogenesis in this region.

The design proposal of "Spices-species" was prototyped through several experiments.

Although, as noted before, the plant interacts with myriad beings, the design of the proposal focused on the plant's main pollinators: carpenter bees of the genus *Xylocopa* (Fig. 2.6).

We sketched, modelled, and prototyped several versions to create what we call a "cycle initiator." The intention was to create

FIGURE 2.6 Two visitors. Above: leaf-footed bug (*Coreidae* family). Below: main pollinator, carpenter bee (species *Xylocopa*), taking nectar, note the pollen collected on its back. (Photo by Leonardo López)

a device that could help to initiate the life cycle of the plant and also provide the housing that enables the nesting of the species *Xylocopa artifex* and *Xylocopa ciliata*. As such, the "cycle initiator" should provide the means by which one can initiate two cycles: that of the plant and that of its main pollinator. At the same time remaining instrumental in its performativity in relation to the human caring for the plant by encouraging a person to use the plant and benefit from its medicinal properties.

The following suggestions form part of the proposal: The set is disassembled and reassembled forming a cane-like structure which is inserted into soil (in a pot or elsewhere in a garden). Then the germinators are planted and watered. The germinators are cylindrical in shape, contain seeds of the passionflower, and are made with vermiculite and clay, which dissolve once watered and allow the soil nutrients to reach the seeds. Once the germinators are planted, it takes on average 30–50 days for the plant to germinate. As it grows, the plant searches with its tendrils for supporting structures on which it can tangle up and climb. The precincts that were first used to pack the parts are now turned into fasteners and a structure for the plant to climb up (Figures 2.7 and 2.8). When

FIGURE 2.7  Cycle initiator set. (Photo by author)

FIGURE 2.8  Starting the cycles through the initiator.
(Photos by author)

the plant has matured and exceeded the height of the initiator it
can be pruned. Pruned parts are placed in a container to make
tinctures. This is done by adding edible alcohol of at least 40%,
and storing in a cool, dark place for between 4 and 8 weeks. After
those 4–8 weeks, leaves and stems are filtered and the tincture is
removed and put into the dosing tube (flask) that comes with the
set (Figs. 2.7–2.9). Taking a dose of tincture has a sedating, relax-
ing effect. The dosage will vary depending on the physical
condition of the person ingesting them, as well as on the quality
of the tinctures produced. Although similar (sedating) effects can
be obtained by directly boiling the parts of the plant in water to
create infusions, we designed the set to encourage the production
of tinctures, being a process less wasteful of the plant and better
than infusions at concentrating its chemicals.

   In the city of Córdoba, there is a lack of plants that these
carpenter bees inhabit and where they build their nests. These

FIGURE 2.9  Procedure to produce tinctures. Bottom
right: flask included in the set. (Photos by author)

plants have the particularity of having hollow stems, for example
cane,[15] thus the need to relate to the passionflower through a
devising that also includes their pollinators and other visitors.
Ideally what we would relate to after a while is something like
what we see in Figure 2.10, if the vital cycles of the plant and the
bees coincide with the installation of the set. Synchronicity is
fundamental.

Importantly, certain beings such as birds and rodents feed
on fruits of plants and disperse their seeds contributing to the
plant's reproduction and increasing "response diversity"[16] which
in ecology refers to "the range of reactions to environmental
change among species contributing to the same ecosystem function."[17] One of the reasons why concern for a wider range of
interactions is of importance, is that this function is critical to
resilience, which is the capacity of a system to deal with change
and continue to develop, and this is especially important during

[15] A more detailed description with images of the plants that these bees inhabit
can be found in Ávila (2017).
[16] I explored the scientific notion of response diversity elsewhere through the
project "Dispersal Machines." See Ávila (2020a).
[17] Elmqvist (2003).

FIGURE 2.10 Female carpenter bee (*Xylocopa*) as it would ideally nest using the set where the passionflower grow. (Photomontage by author)

periods when (eco)systems are under reorganization. If we think of response diversity with the fruits of *Passiflora caerulea* as an example, we could say that this variety of passionflower repro-duces itself by means of the processes of germination that occurs once the fruits fall down on fertile soil (if capable of providing nutrition to the seeds that will, if atmospheric conditions allow, become the new plant). This strategy is complemented by other interactions with other beings. It can be observed in Figure 2.11 that some of these aromatic fruits are pierced, and that they have been partly eaten. What is common is that birds feed on them by piercing the rind to obtain the pulp, and by doing this, the birds swallow a substance that may contain as many as 250 small seeds. Once swallowed, the seeds pass through the digestive tracts of these birds, becoming chemically treated and dissem-inated, depending on the birds that eat them, across some particular spatio-temporal scales through the birds' droppings. The number of species (birds or other) that feed on these fruits varies from plant to plant and from locality to locality. Through

FIGURE 2.11 Fruits of *Passiflora caerulea*, a variety of passionflower. Bird (and other) species feed on these fruits dispersing their seeds. (Photo by author)

this range of responses, the plant continues to reproduce itself in an ecosystem, maintaining certain thermodynamic processes and metabolic flows somewhere, thus influencing the resilience of the ecosystem.[18]

Artificial systems, in order to contribute to resilient ecosystems, must participate and complement this type of multi-scalar ecological relationality across species and adopt cooperative and transversal logics that break away from current linear parameters based on single achievements, such as the optimization of growth of a singular crop, or the consideration of a species in isolation. For this reason, one of the main questions that we have had in mind while conceiving this and other projects and

[18] Thomas Elmqvist and colleagues' comment: "Population fluctuations in a given seed disperser may not have a great effect on the rate of short-distance seed dispersal if a decline in seed dispersal by one species leaves more seeds available for others. An increase in seed availability allows other species to increase their seed dispersal, compensating for the initial decline (a negative covariance effect)." (2003: 490).

their artefacts has been: How can the production of the artificial co-respond materially and rhythmically, to reinforce as many life cycles as possible, to enact and contribute to the dynamics of stable and sustainable ecosystems?

With these complex dynamics in mind, it is clear that there are correspondences between artefactual diversity and biological diversity, and that biological diversity is disappearing at rates only comparable with mass extinctions, due to anthropogenic systems that tend to be based on linear processes and single parameters such as short-term crop yield of few plant species. Hence our suggestions of devices that can attend to the needs of humans in relation to those of local biological actors across scales. As the book unfolds, I will return to these issues in different ways, in Chapter 3 we will revisit this project through the notion of *alter-native*, comparing it to other bee projects that create different material cultures with different possibilities to scaffold the living. Chapter 4 will expand on the ecosemiotic implications of these.

## Doomestics

In this project we focused on domestic environments, the home. Yet, I was interested to work with beings that most people have difficulty cohabiting with, for example, rats, cockroaches, bats, scorpions, spiders, and others. Hence the wordplay "Doomestics" as a working title that frames the tension in the project, expressed by the word "doom," as in a negative destiny, and the domestic perceptual scale of the home.

As in the other projects, we studied several species, mostly guided by the expertise of entomologist Camilo Mattoni, specialist in arthropods (spiders, scorpions). After months of studies and speculations, we decided to work with *Tityus trivittatus* (see Figures 2.12 and 2.13), one of the most common scorpions in Argentina, and the most dangerous to humans in the region. What made this scorpion interesting to us, was the increase of accidental encounters in homes, making it a unique threat in the city. If not treated with an antidote within six hours, the

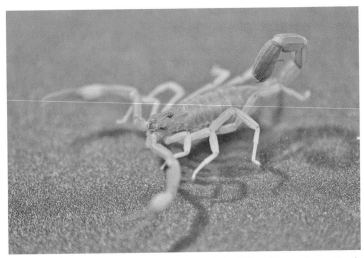

FIGURE 2.12 *Tityus trivitatus* in normal daylight. (Photo by author)

Figure 2.13 *Tityus trivitatus* in UV light. (Photo by author)

scorpion's sting can cause the death of a human child up to six years of age or of people of advanced age or with health problems, the first symptoms of vomiting, sweating and tachycardia appear twenty minutes after being stung.

Scorpions not only find shelter in the sewage system but also opportunities for hunting. The sewers therefore not only perform "as planned," by transporting effluents from buildings, roads, homes, and so on (effluents that disturb our city life and that we don't want in our ordered home environments), they also perform as ecological niches for multiple beings, scorpions included. Cockroaches and mice, to name two of the most common sewer inhabitants, find nutrients accumulated on sewer walls such as sediments of discarded food, blood, semen, and faeces, among many other organic and inorganic substances—which might be harmful or beneficial to a wide variety of organisms that come into contact with these systems. Thus, under the city, and created by the city, we have a thriving habitat for beings that we usually fear and would rather not cohabit with. The scale of their habitat is so vast and these beings are so resilient and pervasive, that we need to contemplate what a responsive cohabitation could mean; not only in a negative sense as a response to a "threat," but also in the positive terms of caring for the liveliness of the environments we inhabit together with scorpions (and rats and others) as species. Denying these ecosystems, and continuously discharging pesticides, which kill indiscriminately, while also poisoning downstream ecosystems, are acts that are not sustainable in the long run.

Besides the accidental encounters with humans, there is also a wider metabolic reality that we consider, by which each individual household of the city is seen as a productive component of an urban metabolism. In other words, are seen as places where things and processes flow through the system and enact ecological possibilities in terms of energy, shelter, nutrition, toxicity, etc. for all actors (a wide range of humans and other-than-humans) that participate in these environments. It is simply not enough therefore to protect the child/human (or the scorpion), but there needs to be a two-way relationship where our actions as human and scorpion contribute towards our co-habitation, a recognition of being of the same city. In our societies most relations to other-than-humans are coded by this unidirectional power (human to others), imposed through technology and territorial occupation. Even if asymmetrical, there is a need for two-way relations of power, to be recognized and materialized in everyday material cultures.

Some of the oldest neighbourhoods of Córdoba are the most affected by the presence of "alacranes" as scorpions are locally known. The food web in these sewers indicates important matters of concern.[19] Decomposers and detritivores such as bacteria, fungi, cockroaches, and other organisms feed on the sediments. Because they break down accumulated materials on the walls, these various "decomposers" are not always undesirable. They find fatty deposits which they metabolize and convert into the components that as proteins and fats make up their own bodies. They also make available inorganic chemicals, which can be recycled as mineral nutrients for plants at the subsequent trophic level, further increasing the consumption of sediments. In this accidental relationship with decomposers and detritivores, there are positive effects for humans since what is waste for us can become food for them. On the negative side, some detritivores, for instance cockroaches, could become vectors for human disease. Additionally, as cockroaches feed and multiply they attract one of the top predators in this food chain: the scorpion.

That scorpions have adapted to living in cities demonstrates their capabilities for survival and indeed thriving, but also highlights our advance into their ecological niches. When it comes to feeding habits, scorpions use their sting to capture prey and defend themselves. They hunt at night and, although they have vision, the vibrations created by their prey also guide their hunting activities; they orient and sense with their whole body. Scorpions do not sting unless provoked or if they feel threatened. Interestingly, our very condition as diurnal human animals has made it difficult to study scorpion ecology. It was not until 1954[20] when the use

---

[19] See Latour (2004: 244).
[20] Polis (1990).

of ultra-violet light became common in field research that their nocturnal habits could be documented and studied (Figure 2.13).

Since *Tityus trivittatus* is potentially deadly for humans, precautions for human safety must be maximized. The idea of cohabiting with them in domestic environments might be discarded automatically, but have they not already adapted to our cities? Are we not constantly expanding our habitats and displacing them and pushing them to adapt to a wide variety of artificial systems? Their adaptability and evolutionary history indicate that they are likely to further adapt to extremes. At present, people are combating them with noxious pesticides, which might be effective in the short term but ecologically devastating in the long term. In most cases, this is complemented by the use of a thin mesh placed under the gratings to stop scorpions from passing through it (Figure 2.14). Although this is effective in terms of prevention of accidental encounters, it maintains the division below/invisible–above/visible without making the natural–artificial continuum liveable. Taking this as an extreme example of the tensions of cohabitation with other-than-humans, the following design, attempts to acknowledge human and scorpion needs at several trophic levels.

This is a proposal for a grating, designed to biodegrade as well as to potentially function as a trap to capture scorpions (Figures 2.15–2.18). The lower, darker part of the grating is made of a clayish mineral compound material, this part does not get in contact with the surfaces of the pipes of the sewage system, leaving two centimetres distance from the inner wall or surface of the pipe. This lower part has a "chamber-like" space that gives it depth (and height) and separates the cavities for the water flows that come from above, from the exterior contours of the device (Figure 2.16). This does not allow cockroaches or scorpions from continuing upwards and come out through the grate. The inside of the chamber however is fitted with adhesive, so if a cockroach or scorpion accidentally gets into the interior of the device, it gets stuck as it steps on the adhesive covering the upper and lower surfaces beneath the grating (Figures 2.16–2.18). In storage, and before using the grating, the glue on the inside is protected and preserved with a sealed strip (Figure 2.15). To

FIGURE 2.14  A standard grate. Note the smaller plastic mesh placed underneath, as recommended by local authorities, to prevent the passage of scorpions. (Photo by author)

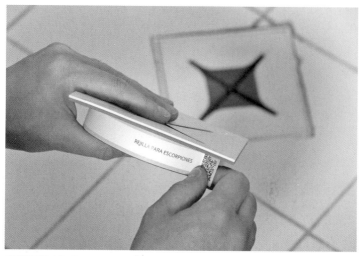

FIGURE 2.15 Opening the protective strip to install a fresh grate and replace the degraded one. (Photo by Fabian Gallucci)

FIGURE 2.16 Left: two grates (one upside down) that show its form. To the right: grate as it fits onto the pipe of the sewage. Notice the gap between the pipe walls and the chamber. (Rendering by author).

FIGURE 2.17  The inside chamber is adhesive and traps individual scorpions or cockroaches if they try to get into it. (Photo by Fabian Gallucci)

FIGURE 2.18  Taking away the degraded grate. (Photo by Fabian Gallucci)

install the grating, the strip must first be removed (Figure 2.17). The grating is then placed on the outlet pipe and it is immediately functional. The use of the shower will create a water flow that slowly degrades a white mineral layer on the grating's upper and visible side. Successive showers gradually reveal a darker layer underneath, made of the clayish mineral compound and will become increasingly more visible (compare Figures 2.15 and 2.19). The incremental darkening is a way for the grating to signal decay and transformation, and to warn us humans that we are becoming more and more "exposed" as we come into closer connection with the sewer.

In contrast to the fixed (metal or plastic) grating between the "underworld" and us, our device operates to expose and not "hide" the sewer. It makes apparent the need to maintain the system with the intent to transform our relationship to the "underworld" of sewage. In practice, there is thus a need to maintain the gratings by replacing them once they darken and visually signal a "connection" to the sewer. If the shower is used frequently, the device is designed to degrade in approximately three to four months. Once degraded, the user replaces the grating and discards it: it might be composted; it might be directly mixed with soil, or just thrown in the garbage bin. If cockroaches or scorpions have been trapped, the nutrients that have been accumulated by catching them on the sticky surface are all part of the device and can be re-inserted into biophysical cycles. Since the grating's materials continue to degrade, it is up to the person to let the artefact contribute to some visible living cycle nearby or not. By scanning a QR code with a mobile device, the user would also get information on how to use, install, maintain, and recycle the grating (Figure 2.15). During its useful cycle (when operating as a grating), the device would complement natural processes by releasing non-toxic organic and inorganic materials. This would increase the sense of connection rather than of division with those places and systems that we do not see.

In their own way the three projects presented here have attempted to make sense of different actors, at different scales, with the ambition to become accountable, responsive and responsible, to at least a few of those beings that we encountered.

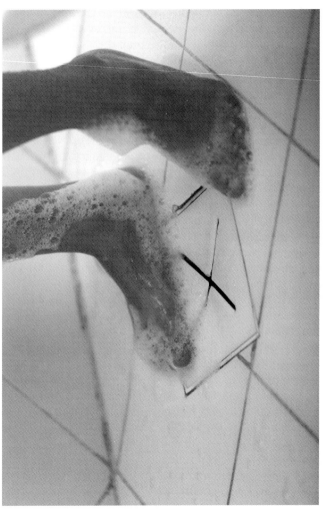

FIGURE 2.19  Grate while showering. (Photo by Fabian Gallucci)

The projects "¡Pestes!", "Spices–species," and "Doomestics" suggest alternative possibilities for relating to different creatures and each of them devises degrees of control in relation to them. The projects, beside attempting to appeal to multiple senses, also strived to scaffold the living, with the idea to increase the possibilities to engage in inter- and intra-action[21] with other beings. This has certainly led to paradoxical proposals by which, for example—and in order to protect species that inhabit and relate to sewage systems—certain individual members of species (in this case scorpions and cockroaches) risk being killed if relating directly to the device we designed. However, we have to stay within the paradoxes and work with the tensions of the devising, never settled, never purely beneficial or harmful in general, only beneficial or harmful in relation to the specificity of the relations they enable. Avoiding the dualistic thought and the dichotomies harmful–benefit, construction–destruction, natural–artificial, life–death, and so on, we have to pursue the work of caring and develop "pharmacological skills", attending to how something, depending on dose and use, may became poison or remedy (see "Grounded semiosphere" in Chapter 4). Attending in this way to how our mattering through design becomes both, constructive *and* destructive in more-than-human ecologies. This is a basic and necessary step towards enacting a life-affirming culture of design. Part of the task is to displace *the scale of control*; from the anthropocentric to the ecocentric, by which we, as species, become better attuned to myriad beings which the practice of designing in the current paradigm has rendered invisible.

---

[21] As noted, "Agency is not an attribute but the ongoing reconfigurings of the world." Barad (2007: 141). We are always in the middle. In this sense, Karen Barad's notion of intra-action folds on Stenger's ecology of practices as instances of Gilles Deleuze's and Félix Guattari's thinking "par le milieu," both the middle and the habitat, without an ideal horizon. Equally, a biose-miotic/ecosemiotic approach pursues this "middle," Maran writes "environmental signs cannot be viewed solely as projections of an organ-ism's cognition to the environment nor can they be approached as objective properties of the environment. Rather, environmental signs appear where the qualities of the environment and the animal's meaning-making activities meet." (2020: 6).

Paradoxically in this shift, at the same time, the loosening of control is required, and it involves situated responses and not abstract ones, risky in different degrees and always with the life of some at stake.

Having introduced these three projects, the pages that follow are considerations folded onto, or considerations that depart from, these speculations through design.

## NOTES ON NOTICING SCALES

Through the basic categories of "space" and "time," the diagrams of Figure 2.20 map part of the designing and thinking processes of "Spices–species" and "Doomestics," as we tried to be explicit about the information gathered from different sources and to visualize for ourselves in an effort to engage in some kind of cartographical sense-making. The information presented is based on discussions with specialists, as well as people in different kind of relations to the projects as they unfolded. The diagram was produced in different phases, and it was used first to ideate and understand what we were collecting, to discuss different implications while trying to make sense of those broken links that our propositions could relate to as well as those that we could not manage to acknowledge through the devising.

The word "intra" on the top left side refers to the scale itself of the project, where the focus was on the "intra" level of ingesting chemicals from a plant for medicinal purposes.[22] What is annotated in terms of time (one year) and space (one kilometre) is the average capacity of the beings that we were studying to live and the average capacity to displace themselves. In this way, we were visualizing for ourselves, and even to communicate with those we worked with, the possibilities to think issues such as response diversity across species and scales. It is interesting to note the difficulty of

[22] These two projects were developed together with a third project that is not presented here. Each of these worked at a particular scale in relation to human bodies, ranging from the "intra" to the "inter" and the "extra."

assigning an average lifetime to the passionflower since, as a plant, the categories of individual/collective/offspring blurs.[23] In spite of this, we assigned the temporal average of seven years to the passionflower, following specialists who asserted that this is the period when the same "individual" could be identified.

What other beings were there, not listed in this basic mapping, which may be important to understand ecological interdependencies? I will revisit a concern raised throughout these projects, namely, that we are always choosing, consciously or not, *some others*. Which are the others that these projects have paid most attention to?

## LIMINAL CREATURES

There are many artefacts that have been designed for other-than-human beings, for example: bird feeders, bat houses, dog kennels, and cat doors to name some of the most common ones close to domestic environments. At urbanistic scales, motorways have started to incorporate passages for wild animals and in cities, green corridors are started to be considered as part of the established parameters for city planning procedures, to name a few. Following political philosophers Sue Donaldson and Will Kymlicka, and in order to be more specific about the kind of work presented in the book, I will distinguish between domestic, liminal, and wild animals.[24] Donaldson and Kymlicka remind us that domesticated animals, those selected to live amongst us on the one hand, and wild animals, those living out in the wilderness

---

[23] In relation to plants, Michael Marder writes "The difficulty . . . lies in the ambiguity of the concept of individuality, which at the same time singularizes and generalizes the entity it comes to describe." Marder (2013: 50).

[24] Donaldson and Kymlicka (2011). There are innumerable degrees of relations with animals, in their species-specific possibilities with humans, and in a wide range of power asymmetries. See also the work of Donna Haraway, particularly Haraway's *The Companion Species Manifesto*. An elaboration of Donaldson and Kymlicka's work as well as a critique of aspects of Haraway's work can be found in Meijer (2019).

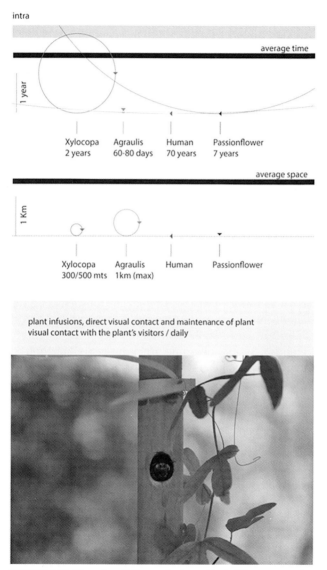

FIGURE 2.20 Mapping different beings (their life-spans and movement possibilities) through space and time coordinates. (Illustration by author)

inter

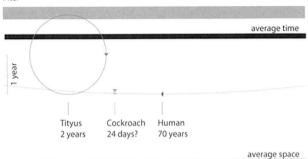

average time

1 year

Tityus
2 years

Cockroach
24 days?

Human
70 years

average space

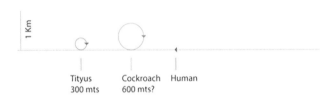

1 Km

Tityus
300 mts

Cockroach
600 mts?

Human

tactile contact, visual contact through the degrading process / daily

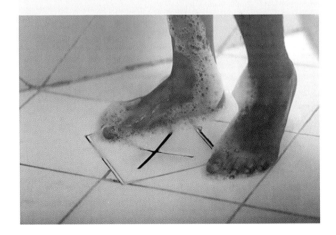

of forest, sky, and ocean on the other, form a domestic–wild dichotomy that in the popular imagination encompasses all animals, but "which ignores the vast numbers of wild animals who live amongst us"[25] that is to say, liminal creatures.

The word *liminal* stems from the Latin word *limen*, which means threshold. What is liminal is somewhere between wild and domestic, and as such exist at the threshold between these states of relation with humans. A variety of humans relate differently to a variety of other-than-human and create multiple degrees of naturecultures. An arthropod like the scorpion that we have discussed previously, is an example of such an animal, living at the threshold of human domestic spaces and inhabiting the affordances of the marginal environments and effluents of certain human cultures. But there are countless others, including rats, foxes, iguanas, squirrels, pigeons, sparrows, deer, and many more that have adapted to the modified environments of urban ecologies and agroecosystems. It is important to keep in mind that the categories of domestic, liminal, and wild, as most categories discussed in this book (human, species . . .) are fuzzy and have many overlaps. They should be understood as shorthand for a provisional identification of relations of dependency and independency with human beings, keeping in mind that these are cultural conceptions as well as ecological categories.

Dog kennels, cat playgrounds, or cat doors are part of the most common repertoire of a material culture that acknowledges cohabitation with animals, these are those exceptional cases where humans have co-adapted and found companion species that intimately relate to us in our homes, what we call domestic animals. The projects featured in this book, however, bring to the forefront the need to recognize and acknowledge liminal animals, while supporting the position that wild animals require territorial protection and are thus dependent on us for conservation efforts and natural reserves. This does not exclude that we have to also recognize the occasional presence of wild animals in human settlements while understanding that there is

[25] Donaldson and Kymlicka (2011: 210).

no wilderness in an absolute sense, only in degrees of relation to global systems affected by human development.

## VISIBLE PATTERNS

Apart from the relatively few artefacts designed to cohabit with domestic animals, for the most part, the devices that are directly in contact with our bodies or our houses, do not intentionally host other species, quite the opposite. We keep on maintaining separations, a distancing that creates invisibility, and a lack of recognition that makes it difficult to empathise with other species. This led to a culture that combines what Val Plumwood has called *backgrounding*, the systematic ignoring of considerations about "nature"; *remoteness*, which is a result of poor feedback links and have temporal, spatial, and technological dimensions; *instrumentalization*, the anthropocentric use of "nature" as "resource"; and *disengagement*, the ignoring of environmental problems by appearing rational.[26] Donaldson and Kymlicka mention,

> Much has been written about the invisibility of domestic animals in modern society. A casual glance at a nineteenth-century newspaper underscores the change—the papers are filled with accounts of "unruly" cows and pigs running amok in towns and cities. The history of industrialized agriculture is a history of the gradual separation of domesticated animals from human spaces—increasing restriction and confinement, and gradual removal of animals from the centre to the periphery of urban areas. Cities and towns have passed ever more restrictive by-laws to regulate domesticated animal bodies, including animal companions.[27]

[26] See Plumwood (2002) To this list of four aspects presented by Plumwood, visual communication lecturer Johanna Boenhert adds a fifth one, *quantitative reasoning*, where "to know" becomes equivalent to "quantify," at the expense of other forms of knowing. For an overview of these see Boehnert (2018: 58-59).

[27] Donaldson and Kymlicka (2011: 113).

In this context, we have been successful at controlling most visible beings outside of our homes, but not as successful with the invisible ones. It is known that different clothing or that different forms of showerheads will create environments for hosting different type of bacteria[28] and, in different degrees, the same applies to furniture and even to electronic products—the seemingly most sterile of the products found at home. Bacterial life is something that we cannot completely control, completely exclude, and even if it would be possible, it would not be desirable. The composite organisms called humans are the result of symbiogenesis, the evolution of species by symbiosis, and the partnership with microorganisms is the oldest one.[29] Not even hospital ecologies benefit from a total eradication of bacteria, a reason why new initiatives study and cultivate nonpathogenic bacteria in these environments.[30]

Architecture can be said to be the inscription of partitions,[31] the devising by means of walls, windows, roofs, that divide to exclude most and control temperature and weather to suit human needs. This is understandable and even necessary in order to develop personally without the struggle for survival in the face of adversity. Yet, by pushing this form of control by excluding most other beings, even those that are not directly threatening in any way we incur in a destructive pattern. Gregory Bateson wrote:

> I suggest that the last 100 years or so have demonstrated empirically that if an organism or aggregate of organisms sets to work with a focus on its own survival and thinks that is the way to select its adaptive moves, its "progress" end up with a destroyed environment. If an organism ends up destroying its environment, it has in fact destroyed itself.[32]

[28] Dunn (2018).

[29] See https://www.ncbi.nlm.nih.gov/pmc/articles/PMC4080534/. For a history of symbiosis see Margulis (1998). Also, Margulis and Sagan (2007). For a summary overview see Sagan (2011).

[30] See for example Arnold (2014).

[31] Grosz (2008).

[32] Bateson (2000[1972]: 457).

Thus, paraphrasing Bateson, we incur in the destructive practice of focusing on our own survival and thinking that that is the way to adapt and "progress," while in fact is a recipe for the destruction of our environments, and thus of ourselves.

By gaining control over the lives of others in parallel to the mastering and tapping onto thermodynamic processes, we transitioned into these early decades of the twenty-first century by replacing animals with machines. In this way, in Eurocentric cultures, it became possible to transport ourselves by replacing horses—animals which were often a "disruptive workforce"[33]— with the more "obedient" cars. I am not suggesting a nostalgic historical view of the relation to horses as means of transport, what I am interested here is to understand the signifying chains that are operative when we control different materials (biological, geological), and the ecologies of practice they enact. With this control we disassociated from the environments which provided the materials for the production and sustenance of horses as means of transport with the resulting invisibility and silencing of animal agency.[34] With this control we also dissociated not only from the relation to the power, fear, joy, stress, beauty, and pain of horses, but also from the material and energy flows relating to horses in captivity: relations to plants used for foraging and in this way to the soil, pollinators, and many others that enact their ecology. For example, the direct relation to the signs of effort (sweat, heat, slowness . . .) in contact with the horses, and the direct relation with the excretions and reproductive cycles of their bodies. Signs that indicated limits to interactions, signs that may trigger responses to living creatures in and with a given context, signs of phenomena that form part of the lifecycles of multiple species.

Parallel to this period of disassociation from the signs of life that involved the relating to these animals, we started to disassociate from the material means that would make it possible to relate to the material ecologies of machines such as cars, due to the global character of their production. The extraction of metal,

[33] Donaldson and Kymlicka (2011: 115).
[34] See Meijer (2019: 185).

rubber, oil, and the many other materials that form part of such machines were not visible in the cities where most people utilized them. The signs in the jungles, the mountains, the oceans and in all the places where the extraction of these took place were not part of the visions of progress of a global capitalist-industrial complex. Disengaging humans in cities across the planet, the signs of life of this dominant culture only correspond to (a few) human social visions where "nature" is backgrounded, signs no longer or poorly attuned to respond to the myriad manifestation of needs of other-than-human beings.

This signifying activity is what Jesper Hoffmeyer describes as *semiotic fitness*, which is "the optimized organism-environment relation" in this relation, the parameters are "the magnitude of the flow of energy and the semiotic controls guiding the utilization of that energy—that have constituted the pivotal points in the historical project of civilization, and in the evolution of life on earth."[35] In Hoffmeyer's view, the current "disproportion between our semiotic and our energetic command of natural systems is the key to the lack of sustainability of industrial and agricultural production."[36] In this sense it is interesting to notice the remarkable effort (energy, materials) to maintain the most common domestic animals, dogs and cats, partly due to their dependency on us for food, food that needs to be procured in abstraction, from supermarkets disconnected from local ecologies, while these animals, predominantly cats, decimate the local

---

[35] Hoffmeyer (2008a: 345). This was observed in the nineteeth century by Karl Marx as the "irreparable rift in the interdependent process of social metabolism" (Marx, 1981: 949). In the context of design, John Thackara has worked with the notion of *metabolic rift* (coined by John Bellamy Foster and inspired by Marx) through projects that address bioregionalisms and the "urban-rural divide". See: http://thackara.com. For a thermodynamic explanation of life processes see Schneider and Sagan 2005).

[36] Hoffmeyer (2008a: 345, note 5). If we think of semiotic links to environments in the context of electric products, Thomas Thwaites' "Toaster project" can be seen as an effort to relink lost semiotic bonds to the contexts from where materials are extracted and, in this way, how they relate to the parts of the semiosphere affected in those locations. See https://www.thomasthwaites.com/the-toaster-project/

populations of animals (birds, mice, etc.) that participate in ecose-miotic and thermodynamic processes and are indispensable actors in local ecosystems.

To get a sense of the pervasiveness of this anthropocentric devising that results in the controlled environments that disrupt semiotic possibilities of relation, I present a basic diagram—through the series of Figures 2.21–23—that places a few artefacts in relation to a scheme where the parameters are *control* (or lack of it) and *threat* (or absence of it). It puts the life of humans as "measure," to generalize about threats that may be perceived psychologically and/or physically. Each of the artefacts presen-ted in the diagrams are positioned along these axes, with a circle that has a shade that suggests degrees of relation to other-than-humans. These range from "wild" to "domestic," going through "liminal," and may help understanding aspects of cohabitation with other-than-humans, particularly animals. The simplifications of the diagrams that follow, are merely a starting point to visu-alize a scheme that could help us provisionally speak of these differences. They also point at the homogenising tendencies of the current design paradigm, which through artefacts conceived without knowledge of the multiple localities where these arte-facts will be used, tend to erase human and other-than-human diversity in the places where they live.

When we are confronted with a scorpion in the shower, or bacteria in our clothes, we understand that these creatures are in our domestic habitats because we have not succeeded at excluding them or have not had the need to do so.

Furniture, clothes, and electronic devices (the most common artefacts in domestic environments), could be placed at the lower right corner of Figure 2.21, based on varying degrees of bacterial activity.

As we recognize other beings in our designs we move away from the bottom corner on the right side since we diminish control, by creating devices that are compromises shaped by what we understand to be the interests of different beings (Figures 2.22 and 2.23). The anthropocentrism of devising becomes de-centred and degrees of ecocentrism are enacted through such compos-itions, giving importance to the unknowns of relating to other

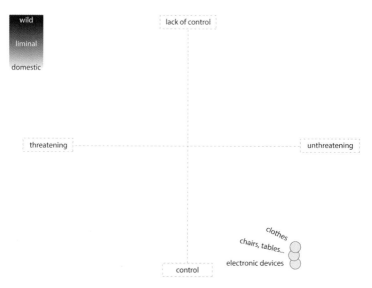

FIGURE 2.21  Controlling threat. A few domestic artefacts.

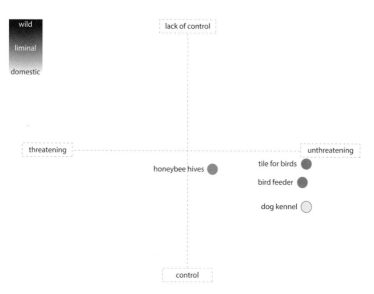

FIGURE 2.22  Controlling threat. A few artefacts designed for other-than-humans.

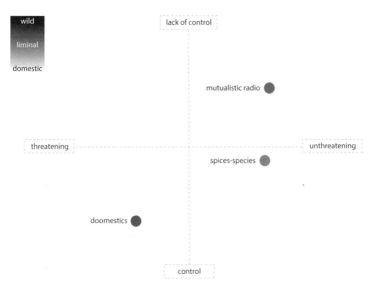

FIGURE 2.23 Controlling threat. Mutualistic radio; Spices-species; Doomestics.

beings, uncertainties materialized to afford engagement. By acknowledging other beings, we are also acknowledging their presence, their modes of being, their capabilities and, potentially, their rights[37] alongside human beings to enact the biosphere in reciprocal intra-activity.

[37] The pioneering constitutions of Ecuador (2008) and Bolivia (2009) based on indigenous cosmogonies and "concepts" such as *Pachamama* (translated as "world mother" or "mother earth") and *sumak kawsay* (translated as "good living" or "good life") were the first nation states to give "rights to nature." Reflections on the legal implications of these can be found in Zaffaroni (2015). From a liberal democratic tradition, animal rights' advocates continue to theorize relations of coexistence with animals from a different frame for moral justice, for example through Citizenship Theory approaches, as in the case of Donaldson and Kymlicka's *Zoopolis*. For a critique of *Zoopolis* see: Edmundson (2015: 749–765). See also Meijer (2019). I believe that these two strands (animal ethics based on liberal democratic traditions, and ecological ethics based on traditional ecological knowledges) are based on seeing different patterns that result in different ethical relations to beings and environments, what Freya Matthews describes, in a more specific sense, as the difference between Axial ethics and Deontic ethics. See Mathews (2012: 114–131).

## COMMONING

Much flora and fauna remain invisible through design, the act itself of recognition and incorporation of consideration in our designs due to their presence becomes a most basic sense of participation. This act of recognition and inclusion by designing can be seen as an activity of commoning, that is, as an effort to managing a commons, such as a local ecosystem. Yet the practices of commoning are different, operate at different scales, and the "managing" involves the enaction of an ecosystem by multiple species, not only humans. A carpenter bee's interest in the pollination of passionflowers has to do with its interest in the flower affording food. Bees and humans may share interest in the plants but participate in the enaction of the ecosystem in ways that diverge.

What brings us (human and bee) together is "an interest in common that is not the same interest" as anthropologists Mario Blaser and Marisol De La Cadena mention. Even though their focus is primarily on human interests in relation to varying human cosmogonies, I believe that it is possible to follow this reasoning across species and agree with them that "Accepting that we (those involved in commoning) may not be metaphysically committed to a common world but rather to going on together in divergence."[38] Perhaps the wording should be changed when thinking of interspecies relations, thus we could write "may not be *ontologically* committed to a common world" instead. Commoning seen in this way is enacted in tension, by ecologies of practice across species, across ontologies, across capabilities, across worlds. A commoning that acknowledges that what is at stake is the enactment of enlivenment through the artificial and thus, a commoning that actively participates in the semiosphere, producing material cultures where artefacts diversify by attending to

[38] See Blaser and Cadena (2017: 191–192). Following Blaser and Cadena, commoning involves "domaining" and thus "constitutes sites where uncommonalities abound" (p.187). See also Marisol De La Cadena's work with the notion of divergence in Cadena (2015). Also Cadena (2019).

the multiplicity of the signs of life in the many places where it will be practiced.

In the following chapter we will situate this perspective in relation to the dominant design paradigm and contextualize it through the implications of some projects by designers that include other species in their devising.

# 3  Alter-natives

[A]ll organisms human and nonhuman *expect the Earth*. We
are made in it, and remade in each generation in that expectant
relation to things. For us in our material presence, we expect
things that have not yet come to be, but which wait to enfold
us. Thereby we arrive to become opened up to further, a
lifetime's, relations.
*Expecting the Earth*, WENDY WHEELER

And seeking, here, means, in the first place, creating,
creating a life "after economic growth," a life that explores
connections with new powers of acting, feeling, imagining,
and thinking.
*In Catastrophic Times*, ISABELLE STENGERS

## ALTERNATIVES AND ALTER-NATIVES

How to name these searches for alternative propositions?
What words could help understanding design as a poetics of
relating that engages in cross-species sense making? Perhaps a
hyphen in the word alternative can help framing these questions,
and instead of talking about alternatives we may speak of
*alter-natives*.

I suggest that by using the word *alter-native* to describe
artefacts' relations to environments and beings, one indicates
the *alterity* of a thing, its own foreignness to environments

by being artificial, fabricated by humans. Naming something alter-native also demands thinking how some-thing *alters* the relations to those that live in an environment, how it makes them different in some way. An alterity which additionally demands thinking how these things may be designed for co-adaptation by acknowledging the capabilities of multiple species. Through these ongoing considerations, the notion of alter-natives can help us to conceive artefacts that are alternatives to the current paradigm of artefacts conceived and designed without attention to the ecological realities of the places where they will be constructed, used, or discarded. As such, what may be understood as alter-natives are artefacts that to the highest possible degree participate in the affirmation of life processes, as opposed to most artefacts which, despite their concreteness as material devices, create abstraction to the living and by means of their very global character claim to "function" in any environment.

Yet, it is not strictly the global character of these artefacts that is threatening life systems, rather it is the erasure of the localities and the biotic links by means of the lack of recognition of the biophysical realities of the different places where these artefacts are produced, used, and discarded. Artefacts may still be coupled to global material streams, if the global network of actors that provide the product-service-system manages to affirm the biophysical constraints through the relations of the product and by-products that affect the local ecosystems at the different stages of its life cycle, from production to discard.

The category *alter-natives* refers only to the status of artefacts produced by humans, addressing how varying responses at different scales relate to locations as they participate, or not, in the enlivening of those places. In this sense the notion of *alter-natives* is related and complementary to Val Plumwood's concept of *shadow places*, that is, the places that provide our material and ecological support, which in a global economy are places that often become "shadowed," "south" places that stand in contrast to "north" places which tend to become idealized places of belonging. Plumwood writes:

Ostensibly place-sensitive positions like bioregionalism evade rather than resolve the problem of the split by focussing exclusively on singular self-sufficient communities, thus substituting a simplistic ideal of atomic places for recognition of the multiple, complex network of places that supports our lives. If being is always being towards the other, the atomism and hyper-separation of self-sufficiency is never a good basic assumption, for individuals or for communities. Communities should always be imagined as in relationship to others, particularly downstream communities, rather than as singular and self-sufficient. An ecological re-conception of dwelling has to include a justice perspective and be able to recognise the shadow places, not just the ones we love, admire or find nice to look at.[1]

By striving to produce *alter-natives* that participate in the semiosphere and thus in ecological processes, material cultures may emerge where artefacts diversify by attending to the multiplicity of the signs of life, rather than to the unidirectionality of financial interests or the unilateral inertia of human performativity. Since what is at stake is the reworkings of a dominant material culture that has become synonymous with consumption (product design), it is of particular importance to frame the effort to conceive artefacts as alter-natives, as a critical approach that "must aim to replace the consumer-driven narratives of place that mark our lives by different ones that make our ecological relationships visible and accountable."[2]

Using design researcher Johan Redström's diagram[3] (Figure 3.1) one could visualize, simplifying and in generic terms, what the current devising paradigm implies if we compare it with a ecocentric paradigm that pursues to develop *alter-natives* as a goal for interspecies cohabitation (Figure 3.2).

---

[1] Plumwood (2008) I am thankful to Thomas Laurien for pointing me at the complementarity of the notion of shadow places and alter-natives.

[2] Plumwood (2008: 140).

[3] Redström (2017) For accounts of "from where" (in Redström's diagram) histories of design have been narrated and potential for alternative narratives, see Göransdotter (2020).

FIGURE 3.1  Based on Johan Redström's *Making Design Theory*. (Illustration by author, based on Redström 2017:39)

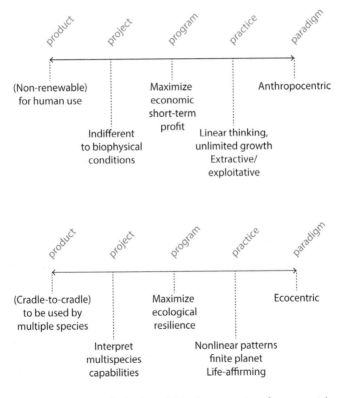

FIGURE 3.2  Above, designing within the current anthropocentric paradigm. Below, designing within an ecocentric paradigm. (Illustrations by author)

Choosing to ask whether devices can be alter-natives demands unfolding whether that happens, how that happens, when, where, and for whom that may be. The notion of alter-natives does not explain, does not explicate; it demands answers, specific, situated answers, the implications need to be unfolded, traced, maintained, and actualized.

By highlighting the word "native" with the hyphen I am not suggesting a binary and simplified opposition native-alien. To strive to become alter-native does not mean to claim "nativity," "indigeneity," or "endemicity," rather, it is a process of getting to or towards "nativization," "indigenization," or "endemization" through a search that attempts to affirm the possibilities of behaviour of those that live in a given place, some of which may be unique to the environment (endemic or indigenous), while others may be natives or even foreigners to the places they inhabit.[4]

What is at stake is the enactment of enlivenment through the artificial. While humans and many other species are generalists (to varying degrees), numerous species are specialists and have co-evolved through specific relations with other species of the places they inhabit, developing co-dependencies and unique forms and processes in response. These niched capacities make them vulnerable when local differences are not recognized. It is in relation to these vulnerabilities when the work of affirmation may lead to enlivening compositions.[5]

## CASES OF MAKING WITH, FOR, OF . . . BEES

Continuing with the "Spices-species" project as well as some projects by Marlène Huissoud, Clive van Heerden and Jack Mama,

[4] The complexity of the political work relating to ecological activity demands situated responses to assess the threats to local fauna and flora by introduced species that may become invasive. Often at stake are different knowledges validated by differing practices and worldviews. For colonial patterns in ecological work see Anker (2001). In urban contexts, see Ernstson and Sörlin (2019). Also, Ernstson and Swyngedouw (2019). See also Freja Mathews' account of conflicting ethics in wildlife conservation (2012).
[5] For a discussion of ethics of response as "composition" see Hoppe (2019).

and Neri Oxman, we will explore the concept of *alter-natives* in some empirical examples looking in the first instance at how some projects enact possibilities of relationship with bees.

Bees are important since they pollinate about a sixth of the flowering plant species of the world and about 400 different types of agricultural plants. This makes them the most important insects to humans, but also to all kind of beings since plants are the first link in food chains.[6] As mentioned earlier on, it is common to associate bees with beekeeping or apiculture, activity that started about 9000 years ago in Northern Africa, which in present days is characterised by the global maintenance of the population of *Apis mellifera*, a species native of Europe, the Middle East, and Northern Africa.

If we consider the traditional tools used in beekeeping through this global industry, how do we consider the designed artefacts such as the box and parts for hives (wooden) or the smoker (metal), as *alter-natives*? As mentioned, the notion of alter-natives does not explain, it demands answers, specific, situated answers. To try to answer how the tools for apiculture may be analysed through the notion of alter-natives, it will require the contextualization in a particular place, and making sense of the place's infrastructure, ecological conditions, biodiversity, geo-political histories, and so on.

There are no shortcuts. For example, if we were to pay attention in general to the materials that these are built with, they are quite likely from other parts of the world than those where they are used, although they may be able to be recycled or biodegraded in these places. So even though we may consider this as a first aspect to think about the possibility of these tools to participate in local biological or industrial cycles, we can only speculate. Yet through speculation one may find new questions that demand answers and allow us to gain understanding towards the tasks of designing.

Besides the material flows, other questions should concern biodiversity: Are the bees that they introduce and reproduce

[6] See https://www.onegreenplanet.org/animalsandnature/why-bees-are-important-to-our-planet/. Accessed June 21, 2021.

alien to the ecosystems where they are introduced? If so, these may compete with local varieties of bees and other pollinators if there are not enough available plants or if the plants are of the same kind. At the same time, if there are available plants and plants of different kinds, then the introduction of bees may not compete with the local varieties of bees and may increase the pollination of plants in the nearby areas.

Two other aspects to consider: On the one hand, whether the bees are kept for pollination purposes and not for harvesting honey (or to what extent a combination of these is happening), and on the other hand, the scale of beekeeping, since the monocultures of plants that demand pollination from commercial beekeeping disrupt ecological resilience.[7] Understanding that the primary function of the combination of these tools (hive and smoker) is to facilitate the collection of the honey produced by the bees, we can assume that these artefacts maintain the instrumental hierarchy in which humans control and dominate, primarily for humans to consume the honey (which is food made by bees and it is intended to be used by bees as store of food for the winter). Bees create this food, honey, by extracting nectar from flowers, then regurgitating the nectar and passing it back and forth in their mouths to one another until they deposit and seal it in a honeycomb.[8]

With these considerations it is possible to start appreciating the complexity of the inter and intra actions of a material culture in relation to these beings. Biodiversity and consideration of the scales at which the artefact affects an ecosystem are central, and cradle-to-cradle principles must participate in the ecological cycles of the environments where these devices may become alter-natives to those others that live and depend on the available food chains of the region.

If bees are kept in small numbers and biodiverse areas, ecologies of care for bees, the plants that they pollinate, birds that feed

---

[7] See for example the case of almond pollinating in the USA: https://www.theguardian.com/environment/2020/jan/07/honeybees-deaths-almonds-hives-aoe. Accessed June 21, 2021.

[8] See https://theecologist.org/2019/aug/21/eating-honey-bad-bees. Accessed June 21, 2021.

on bees (depending on the region), and humans may be maintained. This doesn't exclude the interest that others such as foxes, bears, mice, or hedgehogs may have and may destroy the beekeeping process. If the beekeeping is successful, by respecting the needs of bees, the materials that they produce can be used (if not taken away completely) and will not affect the wellbeing of the bees.

This is what designer Marlène Huissoud did in her project "From Insects" when experimenting with propolis, also called bee glue, which is a sealant produced by honeybees to cover unwanted open spaces in their hive. The material is processed with the saliva of bees and collected from tree resins and sap flows from plant sources. Only about 100 grams of this material is produced per year per hive, making it rare and highly valuable. By working with this precious substance and without interfering with bees' own food production, Huissoud works in partnership with them, encouraging their presence while benefiting from their wellbeing and using propolis to produce unique craft (Figures 3.3 and 3.4).

After purifying propolis by heating it in water until boiling point to get rid of other substances attached to it, the design process with the material started to suggest opportunities: "The propolis was manipulated as a glass but has revealed other properties that gave it unique and unexpected characteristics (colors, texture, facility to manipulate engraved glass)."[9] These characteristics were used to convey aesthetic qualities associated with insects, mimicking patterns and highlighting the value and beauty of insect constructions (Figures 3.3 and 3.4).

To what extent could we think these artefacts as *alter-natives*? The relations are always fragile, giving even more exclusivity or preciousness to the material, since it is believed that propolis also maintains a variety of functions in the hive that would affect the health of the hive.[10] The processes that lead to the production of the pieces make a difference too, for example whether there are chemicals that affect the soil or waterways when making

[9] https://www.marlene-huissoud.com/from-insects. Accessed June 21, 2021.

[10] The Wikipedia entry for propolis mentions seven properties of this material in the hive, including the prevention of diseases and parasites from entering the hive, and to inhibit fungal and bacterial growth. See https://en.wikipedia.org/wiki/Propolis. Accessed June 21, 2021.

FIGURE 3.3 Marlène Huissoud, "From Insects." (Image courtesy of Marlène Huissoud)

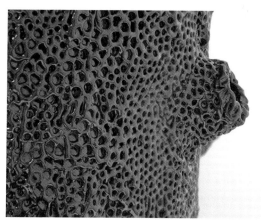

FIGURE 3.4 Marlène Huissoud, "From Insects" Bee vase details. (Photo by Yesenia Tibault Picazo, image courtesy of Marlène Huissoud)

these vessels, or whether the energy utilized for its production comes from renewable sources. Yet, it is through these careful considerations of the fragility and exclusivity of these materials and relations that ecologies of care can be evolved and maintained. Through these careful considerations alter-natives emerge as responses that are compromises with others in relation to the biophysical constraints of a place.

A completely different type of relation with bees is proposed in the projects "Synthetic Apiary" and "Co-Fabrication Systems" by Neri Oxman.[11] Oxman's work explores fabrication with advanced technologies and interaction with different living beings such as silkworms and bees, intending to "enable co-design, co-manufacturing and co-habitation across species."[12] In the project "Synthetic Apiary" (Figures 3.5 and 3.6), Oxman and colleagues are concerned

FIGURE 3.5  Neri Oxman, "Synthetic Apiary." Honeybee hive installation in the Synthetic Apiary environment. (Photo by The Mediated Matter Group, image courtesy of Neri Oxman)

[11] https://oxman.com/projects/synthetic-apiary and https://oxman.com/projects/co-fabrication-systems. Accessed June 21, 2021.
[12] https://oxman.com/projects/co-fabrication-systems. Accessed June 21, 2021.

FIGURE 3.6 Neri Oxman, "Synthetic Apiary." Honeybee hive installation and monitoring in the Synthetic Apiary environment. (Photo by The Mediated Matter Group, image courtesy of Neri Oxman)

with the decline of bees worldwide, a combination of factors that affect bee health such as agricultural pesticides and habitat loss. With this as background, the project:

> explores the possibility of a controlled space in which seasonal honeybees can thrive year-round. Light, humidity, and temperature are engineered to simulate a perpetual spring environment. Bees are provided with synthetic pollen and sugared water and evaluated regularly for health and well-being. In this initial experiment, humans and honeybees co-habitate, enabling natural cultivation in an artificial space across scales, from organism- to building-scale.[13]

The "Synthetic Apiary" is complementary to the project "Co-Fabrication Systems" where they explore construction by different beings.

---

[13] https://oxman.com/projects/synthetic-apiary. Accessed June 21, 2021.

Through this project, by staging artificial daylight conditions, artificial nesting opportunities (box hives), and artificial pollen and fluids, Oxman and colleagues push the bees (*Apis mellifera*) to adapt by simplifying the possibilities of interactions with the environment under laboratory conditions. In this way the work-force and labour[14] of bees is tapped to produce materials and structures for the benefit of humans and, according to the project description, the long-term survival of bees. Here we are immersed in a scenario where the collapse of the bee population is immin-ent, and their maintenance by artificial means is a strategy for co-habitation. In their explorations of form, the resulting co-fabrications are experimental and so are still undefined (as opposed to the particular use of propolis to create a vessel for example). Describing their position, Oxman and colleagues state:

> In Nature—where shape is cheaper than material—one often finds load-resisting structures that combine multiple systems to accommodate for constantly shifting forces over time. Contrary to traditional manmade structural design, where beams and columns are often composed of homogeneous materials, many natural structures exhibit heterogeneity in both shape and material composition.[15]

I would argue, however, that shape is not "cheaper than mater-ial," it has a different temporality, it is more durable than the lives of the individual bees that build the structure. In this sense the negotiation with bees in "Co-Fabrication Systems" are very different since humans are dependent on the bees' capacities to co-form the artefacts to be used. The value of the formation is measured in terms of the duration of the structure rather than the care of the individual bees and is thus the long-term achieve-ment of the continuation of the species and the maintenance of structures for nesting and food storage (in the interest of bee populations rather than individual bees) that constitute the horizon

---

[14] For an account of animal work/labour, see Whitener (2018).
[15] https://oxman.com/projects/co-fabrication-systems. Accessed June 21, 2021.

FIGURE 3.7  Clive van Heerden and Jack
Mama's "Urban Beehive" for Philips
(2010).(Image courtesy of Clive van
Heerden and Jack Mama)

of this vision of cohabitation. Co-adaptation takes a tighter relational dimension, yet humans attempt to keep control and set
the stage.

Another design which explores possible conditions for
beekeeping and the relations of bees and people is Clive van
Heerden and Jack Mama's project "Urban beehive"[16] for Philips
(Figures 3.7 and 3.8). The "Urban beehive" consists of two parts:
An entry passage with a flowerpot on the outside, and a glass
vessel containing honeycomb frames in the inside. It was designed
for keeping bees at home and to allow "a glimpse into the fascinating world of these industrious creatures and to harvest the
honey that they produce." As such, it functions to connect
the outside of a window with the inside of a room, attracting the
bees with the flowers outside and affording the bees to further

[16] https://www.vhmdesignfutures.com/project/78/. Accessed June 21, 2021.

FIGURE 3.8  Clive van Heerden and Jack Mama's "Urban Beehive" for Philips (2010). (Image courtesy of Clive van Heerden and Jack Mama)

navigate the device to build their wax cells by means of the inside frames that possess a honeycomb texture. As in traditional practice, smoke can be released into the hive to calm[17] the bees before it is opened.

How can we think of this artefact as an *alter*-native? The device allows for the placement of different floral plants, facilitating in this way the possibility to attract local species, these

[17] "When bees sense danger, they release an alarm pheromone called isopentyl acetate from a gland near their stingers. This chemical wafts through the air and alerts other bees to be ready to attack. Smoking a beehive masks this pheromone, allowing the beekeeper to safely perform a hive inspection." See: https://www.buddhabeeapiary.com/blog/why-do-beekeepers-use-smoke Also: "In technical terms, the smoke reduces the electroantennograph response of the antennae [. . .] the effect is reversible, and the responsiveness of bees' antennae gradually returns within 10–20 minutes." See: https://www.sciencefocus.com/nature/how-does-smoke-subdue-bees/. Accessed June 21, 2021.

however may not always be honeybee species. For it to function to provide a habitat for honeybees and honey both for bees and humans it will require more floral abundance than the plant that signals the entrance to the potential habitat, something that may encourage gardening in public or other spaces. Besides taking into consideration, as in all cases, what materials are used to produce the device and how these affect the local ecologies where they circulate, it is also relevant to ask, who benefits from this devising? Bees, humans, floral species, birds that may occasionally feed on bees, spiders, other pollinators . . . The instrumental relation with bees through the human interest of obtaining honey may be mutually beneficial if honey is sparingly used, this would allow for the survival of bees during winter, while the inside part in the interior of the human habitat provides warmth to the bees decreasing the need for food during the cold periods. The device is a mediator between an inside and an outside, which is a window to the way bees live; van Heerden and Mama have designed the inside not only for humans to be able to see the interior of the hive but also keeping in mind bees' capacities: "The glass shell of the inside filters light to let through the orange wavelength which bees use for sight."[18] In this sense, considerations of bees' Umwelt have been incorporated into the design and include both the bees and the human's need to see. The partial control over the different dependencies (floral abundance, species' presence, species' capacities) opens up for the acknowledgement of interdependency and thus for thinking degrees of cohabitation with other-than-human species, each human household potentially becoming host for a variety of species and forming a distributed network of socio-ecological opportunities and knowledge.

Returning to the "Spices-species" project, other relations are made possible. The project was concerned with the medicinal use of the passionflower and (by the human interest in that plant) also in their main pollinators, the carpenter bees. Through the project we focused on the non-instrumental relation with the bee, in our case two subspecies of *Xylocopa* (*Xylocopa artifex* and *Xylocopa ciliata*), with the intention to scaffold the ecological

---

[18] https://www.vhmdesignfutures.com/project/78/. Accessed June 21, 2021.

realities of the native flowers that depend on their pollination, as well as the preference of these species for that flower, especially in the city of Córdoba.

Having described the main aspects of this project already, in what way then may this artefact be thought of as an *alternative*? If we consider the materials for the tubular structures that could host the bees, our intention was to work with compound materials obtained from soft woods from trees such as the native silk floss tree (*Ceiba speciosa*). If products like this would be adopted, how often would people need to acquire them? The scale of production and consumption of these artefacts will demand a relation to the local capacity to obtain and process these woods. If the demand is too high the pressure on the ecosystems where these trees exist would increase. Also, as mentioned before, the processes that lead to the production of these pieces may require chemicals that affect the soil or water in destructive ways or require energy from non-renewable sources. These are unknown aspects since the product proposal is not available. Similarly, due to the small scale or experimental character of the other projects that we have investigated (beside the commercial tools for the reproduction of honeybees) it is impossible to assess more concrete degrees of dependencies and interactions. When it comes to the aspect of control however, I would situate them as in Figure 3.9, considering that Neri Oxman's projects experiment with bees and produce results *from* them (maintaining but exploiting them), while Marlène Huissoud's is marginally using them and less able to control what they produce. Clive van Heerden and Jack Mama's Urban beehive is somewhere in between the two considering that they do not control the presence of bees that can inhabit the hive while using it to collect honey. In the case of "spices-species", the bees are not used in any particular way except with the intention that they exist in urban environments and participate in the pollination of these flowers, however, my placing "spices-species" lower in relation to control than Huissoud's project is because of our suggestion of locating the hosting tubular structures beside the plants, which also allows for closer inspection by human beings using or caring for the plant.

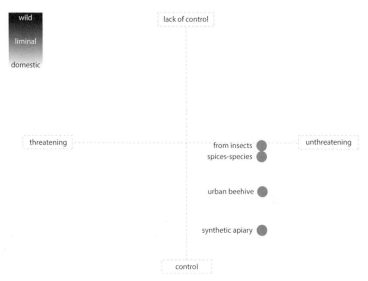

FIGURE 3.9  Controlling threat. Bee-related projects.

Each of the projects has very different potential impact on human and bee populations. In their own particular ways, they attempt to enact ecologies of care for humans in relation to the bees and reconfigure tensions and negotiations with the bees. In the most controlled environment (in Oxman's project) the bees are being pushed to adapt to artificial living conditions and in this way, the prefix "alter" takes another dimension since the scale of the "product" includes the environment where they live. In Huissoud's "For Insects" the scarcity of the material in combination with the design of vessels as one-off pieces of small production scales position it on the opposite spectrum in relation to Oxman's, when thinking of the possibilities of humans to benefit from the labour of bees. Van Heerden and Mama's "Urban beehive" provides the possibility to establish a closer relations with the bees by means of the glass shell in the interior of the building, allowing humans to see the results of the industrious activities of these fascinating creatures. "Spices-species" does not use the bees in any way, yet, like the other projects, it stages a degree of relationship with humans, in which dependencies are created, response-abilities negotiated, and co-adaption required.

## RATS ON THE WALLPAPER

The three projects that have just been presented in relation to bees all have one thing in common: They relate to bees by having previously framed a human need or desire and this sets the conditions and constraints for the type of behaviour of the bees that engage with them. The *anthropos* of which we initially spoke still dominates, even though displaced, in different degrees, from the "centre". Or perhaps still in the centre but not alone. This has consequences not only for the way things are used, but also consequences for the way things look, the aesthetic choices made and traces left on the things themselves.

Following this thinking, it is interesting to consider another project, this time by Front, entitled "Designed by animals"[19] where the designers explored shapes created by animals (rats, snakes, dogs, beetles) and made artefacts for house interiors such as lamps, tables, hangers, or wallpapers from forms or materials "created" or shaped by these animals. In this collection, different things were made by the affordances created by the bodies of animals. For example, a vase was made and casted from the imprints of a dog's leg on the snow (Figure 3.10), or a lamp was made from cavities burrowed by rats. Through these types of explorations there is a reversal; humans build upon the affordances of animal traces. The pigeon does not nest in the pot, it is a person that puts flowers on the cavity left by a dog. The reversal is certainly relative since a great deal of premeditation is required to capture and manufacture such a vase and, following our reasoning, the manufacturing and use of such a piece remains thoroughly anthropocentric; neither dogs nor other creatures benefit from these. Yet, through these pieces there is an opening

[19] http://www.frontdesign.se/design-by-animals-project. Accessed June 21, 2021.

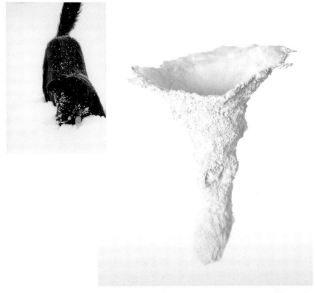

FIGURE 3.10  Front "Dog vase." (Images courtesy of Front)

for an aesthetic of randomness and irregularity which breaks away with the controlled lines of most design projects, and in this basic sense, with part of what may be required to engage in more-than-human modes of creation.

Other things produced in this series include the use of existing artefacts such as tables or wallpapers as food for animals, and thus as a kind of experimental collaboration where the animals fed on the artefacts to the extent where their traces became visible and formed patterns that would give uniqueness to the pieces (Figure 3.11).

In these objects another kind of use of animals emerges, not the one that simply exploits the results of their work but rather one that embraces and welcomes the irregularities of their disruptive (to a human observer) patterning. At least to some extent: If the rats continue eating there is no more wallpaper, and so a next stage of relationship must be incorporated into the process of human production/animal consumption. If these stages where

FIGURE 3.11  Front "Wallpaper by rat." (Image courtesy of Front)

to be developed, where would the rats be hosted? How would they find the wallpapers or other things to feed on?

Many more questions come to mind, and I playfully push for thinking along the possibilities and constraints of this project because design propositions typically require reproducibility and thus responsibility towards those that work (normally humans), creating situations of co-dependency. Even in gestures that at first impression seem generous, degrees of control are required to manage the power asymmetries, the diverging interests of those that participate, the longer- and shorter-term benefits for those that engage and the communities to which they belong.

Through Front's project we can also see and understand other degrees of "co-fabrication" than in Oxman's proposals where, in "Co-Fabrication," the processes of cohabitation with bees and the degree of control and reproducibility that guide the co-patterning is more explicit. Yet, it is not possible to compare the outcomes with the same parameters since the species that they have been working with have very different interests, social

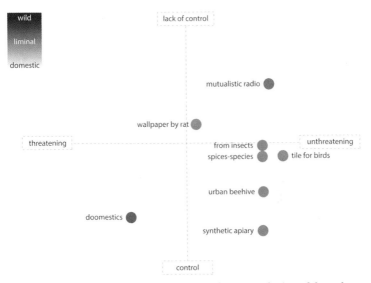

FIGURE 3.12  Controlling threat. Artefacts/projects designed for other-than-humans.

capacities, and scales of action to create patterns that humans may be able to use and recognize.

I return to the diagram that we have been using and place the "Wallpaper by rat" almost in the middle (Figure 3.12), in relation to control slightly higher up towards lack of control since the resulting pattern is random, and in relation to threat almost in the middle as well since the traces left by the rodents may be perceived by some people as potential vectors of disease. Keeping in mind that these diagrams are simply an approximation and an explorative tool, what this positioning makes explicit is that each of the phases, during production, use and discard of an artefact, would require a new positioning. What I have been suggesting considers a few of the relations from a human point of view of the product itself, the wallpaper in this case, but much more information is needed to understand the product through the whole of its lifecycle as it relates to other-than-humans.

By thinking of human-other-than-human relations through artefacts and using the notion of alter-natives, requires responding partially, in the overlaps of interests and semiospheres that can be actualized. One of the interesting aspects of Front's "Designed by animals" is their tapping onto animal traces as affordances for different uses. The playfulness involved in the making of these things still signals the connection to these beings. Their iconic and indexical dimensions induce (seduce?) excitement by pointing at the relation to these creatures; artefacts appreciated for their random patterns, human aesthetic choices that value the traces as other-than-human signs in domestic environments.

We expect the earth and are made and remade in that expectant relation to things as Wendy Wheeler suggests.[20] There are overlaps of interspecies "sense" and sense of play that may be extended, incorporated into everyday life if we attempt to affirm the life of those that relate to the things that we do, through the signs that we produce. Designing, we create some of the things that have not yet come to be, and which wait to enfold us. Interdependence is about dependencies, what does the practice of designing for interdependence depend on? Innumerable things, and certainly, on the joyful search for relating to others, playfully, where designing becomes (de)signing, in search of encounters with signs of life, human and others, to become opened up to further, many lifetimes,' relations.

[20] Wheeler (2016: 212).

# 4  (De)signing Alter-natives

Aliveness is always interweaving dimensions of matter
with perception and experience; it is from the very first cell
rife with those dimensions we normally reserve for culture:
meaning and expression.
*Enlivenment*, ANDREAS WEBER

[W]hile most biologists suppose that *symbiotic mutualism*
is an exceptional case of no general importance for
evolutionary theory, I believe that *semiotic* mutualism
involving a delicate balance of interactions between
many species is widespread.
*Biosemiotics*, JESPER HOFFMEYER

## SCAFFOLDING RELATIONS

Think of the proposals of the projects "¡Pestes!" (mutualistic
radio), "Doomestics" (scorpion grating) and "Spices-species"
(cycle initiator). If the artefacts that we designed were not perceived
by the creatures involved as opportunities for something, then
they were not adopted, by being ignored or simply passed unre-
cognized. At least by those species that we intended to engage.
These devices, whether they afford feeding, being adopted as
refuges, or functioning as traps, must engage those beings by
triggering the perception that certain possibilities exist. Jesper
Hoffmeyer mentions that semiotic scaffolding "is what makes

history matter to an organism (or cultural system)."[1] If those organisms were not able to perceive, could not re-cognize, through their histories of interactions, the new patterns that the artefacts introduced, then our devising failed to understand the signs that these things trigger with, in, and for them.

In the most general sense, the main challenge of all the projects when thinking about human and other-than-human relations, was to identify what semiotic channels were at work in each of them, what signs were introduced and perceived through our propositions. In other words, what *partial connections*, and what part of the *semiosphere* were enacted as these new material propositions, through their expression, triggered new meaning?

This is at the core of what an *alter-native* may be. How does this newness, this other (alter) thing that "emerges" in an environment, participates in the relations of those that live in that environment? Does it degrade and release chemical compounds that affect the soil, air, or water flows? Does it attract visitors of some kind modifying ecological dynamics? Does it engage those humans that relate to it in ways that allow them to participate, through their own cultural practices, in the care for the environment where they live? As environmental philosopher Yogi Hale Hendlin writes, "Histories of symbiosis are cultivated, not merely accidental."[2]

Based on today's "sustainable development goals" in the best cases, the response is to strive to participate in a circular economy, which may contribute to industrial or biological cycles following cradle-to-cradle principles. What is at stake in asking the question of to what extent something can be alter-native, is not to challenge notions of circularity or to present a different model that is not cyclic. It is rather, to challenge and complement the managerialism and quantitative parameters of these models—and in this way, to affirm other-than-human lives, as well as to challenge the perception that "circularity" *per se* is an adequate response while inscribed in an expansive and anthropocentric paradigm.

[1] Hoffmeyer (2015).
[2] Hendlin (2019: 47).

Complementing quantitative parameters, the real task is to bring qualitative, affective dimensions to the circular models, and to understand how devising inscribes partitions that include and exclude relations with living beings at some scale. How devising scaffolds not only through material support but also, how devising scaffolds by inscribing temporal dimensions through the stability of the materials. If the signs are relevant to multiple beings, then they become a frame for learning as Kalevi Kull noted and scaffold histories of interactions with the possibility to adapt and cultivate further relations. Even when considering the biological cycles of the artefacts we devise, it is necessary to attend to the affective relations we are capable to establish and maintain in our near environments through the choices that we make. If every sign is a human sign that points at humans only, if we do not see or hear other creatures, or otherwise feel or perceive their presence, how are we, on an everyday basis, to develop a culture that values and cultivates their existence?

In everyday life, most of us drive more carefully when we see an animal on the road. Where I live it is often deer that I come across. But this carefulness does not only arise from the risk of injury (to the animal, myself, or the vehicle), it also arises from the disruption itself, from the animal's appearance, an "irruption" that grounds us, even if momentarily, on a shared environment. Through this irruption a demand is imposed on us which requires that we negotiate the place where we are. Our mode of operation becomes more attuned to the environmental possibilities; the iconic and indexical dimensions take over symbolic ones[3] and

---

[3] Eduardo Kohn exemplifies this shift (symbolic semiosis nested on icons and indexes) with an example of an occasion when during a trip in Ecuador, a landslide on the road provoked him to feel panic, something that was not shared by fellow passengers, causing a feeling that his thoughts were "out of joint" with those around. Occasioned by abstract associations, this feeling was later in the trip dissipated by the presence of birds: "Watching birds regrounded my thoughts, and by extension my emerging self, by re-creating the semiotic environment in which symbolic reference is itself nested. Through the artifice of my binoculars I became indexically aligned with a

engage us in the recognition of forms and movements that may indicate future actions: Is the deer going to stop in the middle of the road, to run faster, are there other deer? Every single environmental detail indicates alternative possibilities to the situation that I respond to. It is not only up to me, but also up to the deer to respond in such a way as to avoid a collision. Many other factors must be interpreted by both; is there ice or gravel on the road, how fast are we approaching, are there others nearby? Attention is full attention to this, present situation. Learning and adaptive capabilities are nurtured through encounters, the deer may recognize acoustic, visual, or other signs that it may later associate with threat; I may recognize places where deer tend to appear, learn to appreciate nuances of colours among vegetation, or, at an alternative collective scale, the vehicles may incorporate sensors that aid the recognition of their presence.

Not all encounters impose this type of dramatic demands, I am fortunate to often be distracted from my thoughts when I hear a bird singing or a squirrel jumping among the branches of the trees near my house. Living in Stockholm's archipelago, and thanks to its (mostly) open gardens that allow animals to wander, I am privileged to sometimes witness not only deer but also foxes and meet their gaze which scrutinize every single movement of my body to assess the threat that I may be and the possibilities of action in the very spot where they are. I am extra fortunate to witness the rarer comings and goings of elk or the majestic hart which still finds occasional spaces to rest and feed in the denser and denser built environment of the islands. The lives of these beings matter, in different ways, and the detachment caused by devices from all kind of ecosystems imposes challenges to our capacity to empathise, understand, and not least, compromise, in everyday tension with the many that live where we do.

bird, thanks to the fact that I was able to appreciate its image now coming into sharp focus right there in front of me. This reimmersed me in something (. . .) a knowable (and shareable) environment, and the assurance, for the moment, of some sort of existence, tangibly located in a here and now that extended beyond me but of which I too could come to be a part." See Kohn (2013: 57).

## GROUNDED SEMIOSPHERE

A first step to conceive design as a relational ecological practice is to understand design as a signifying activity, a human activity that triggers behavioural possibilities for humans and other-than-humans while enacting and participating in the semiosphere. In this sense and as mentioned, it is useful to work towards a grounding of design constrained by the possibilities of cohabitation with others. The "*ecosemiosphere* is a grounded semiosphere" and it is also how design affects the semiosphere through its indexical and iconic dimensions, con-forming and pointing things out, connecting to "the semiotic fabric of the ecosystem."[4]

The recognition of a semiotic (biosemiotic, ecosemiotic, or a pansemiotic)[5] reality contributes to conceive the practice of design as signifying responses affecting multiple beings and systems, as (de)signing. It helps to explicitly reimagine ecological roles and modes of togetherness, becoming a fundamental part of what Andreas Weber calls ecological poetics; "we can only embrace the paradoxes of lived existence if we allow ourselves

---

[4] Timo Maran speaks of compound environmental signs as possibilities for natural or ecological conventions across species. See Maran (2020: 32). Grounding, as has been suggested throughout the book, has not only semiotic but historical and geopolitical dimensions in relation to ecologies. See Ernstson and Sörlin (2019).

[5] Pansemiotic is the name that Christopher Watkin assigns the "figure of thought" that Michel Serres develops through his philosophy of signification. See Watkin (2020: 258). In spite of the historical distinctions that Watkin makes to differentiate biosemiotics from the "ecosemiotics" or "pansemiotics" of Serres, the current field of ecosemiotics, as in the overview by Maran, already acknowledges and addresses the bio-geo continuum of signification that Serres philosophically proposes, albeit through different approaches and methodologies. Among the several affinities in the approaches of Serres and the field of ecosemiotics is the understanding of correspondences between thermodynamics and life; "information is found in the heart of matter . . . Everything in the universe, humans included, receives, stores, processes and emits information" Watkin quoting Serres, (2020: 258). Hoffmeyer however, expresses that the word pansemiotics "tends to block understanding more than it advances it. (. . .) the project of biosemiotics neither subscribes to nor advances the claim that there is nothing in the world but signs." (2008a: 84).

to think in an embodied fashion, as consciousness in physical form. To think in an embodied fashion is to feel. The language of first-person science is poetic."[6]

Design is the traces of thought. The challenge is to think traces that scaffold the living of most, to use what we can manage to responsibly account for, "we must use nature and at the same time *protect* it in the way we use it."[7] Designing is a paradoxical activity, creating both hospitality and hostility as it unfolds. As such, in its uses, it is capable both of nourishing and poisoning. It is an unstable practice, one that requires pharmacological skill if understood from its etymology, deriving from the word *pharmakon*, meaning "drug" in Greek. Isabelle Stengers writes: "What characterizes the pharmakon is at the same time both its efficacy and its absence of identity. Depending on dose and use it can be both a poison and a remedy."[8] As such, it cannot be dissociated from a context (hence the necessary grounding), from the circumstances that require attention, care, otherwise, paraphrasing Stengers, if we do not pay attention, we provoke the imprudence of an unthinking use, which stabilizes the efficacy as a poison of what is defined as a remedy.[9]

As can be understood from the kind of propositions made throughout the explorations of the design projects of Chapter 2, I am not positioning the human as protector in an act of conservationism, nor positioning the human as a threat to all species, as some kind of being disconnected from the living. Instead, the position is that of a middle range, to be constantly renegotiated in cohabitation with other beings, a compositional responding where humans are part of the processes of life and death, through the enaction that we call "the artificial." In this context the question is, how do we evolve integrated product-service-systems that participate in the cycles of the biosphere and contribute to a more-than-human semiosphere, so that there might be co-adaptive strategies tuned to one another? And which others? (De)signs

[6] Weber (2019: 159).
[7] Weber (2019: 165, emphasis in the original).
[8] Stengers (2015: 100).
[9] Stengers (2015: 101).

materialized and performed to enable responses that sustain the living. (De)signs that re-enact patterns that offer regularities that can become habits for life-affirming behaviour, what Hoffmeyer calls "semethic interaction". The word semethic derives from the Greek *semeion*, sign and *ethos*, habit; Hoffmeyer asserts that:

> Due to the mechanism of semethic interactions, the species of this world have become woven into a fine-meshed global web of semiotic relations. [. . .] these semiotic relations, more than anything else, are responsible for the ongoing stability of Earth's ecological and biogeographical patterns.[10]

The signalling that occurs through our devising in-forms those that encounter these signs and trigger responses. Yet, since each species navigates and enacts its world through their own Umwelts, design is thus required to position itself at the multiple crossings and sense making of interspecies worlds.[11] (De)signing in abstraction without consideration of the local biodiversity where things will be produced, used, or discarded, only re-inscribes abstraction, remoteness, backgrounding and generates shadow places, in short: More ecological devastation. If we take the case of (de)signing under the current global and anthropocentric paradigm we may trace the becoming of an artefact such as a metal grating, that originates in an office in Shanghai, which requires metals from Northern Sweden, to be processed and manufactured in southern China, to later be distributed by ship across the world to be used in Córdoba, Argentina. Through this hypothetical journey, none of the living creatures of any of these places (except for some humans) are part of the sign prescriptions of the

[10] Hoffmeyer (2008a: 189–190). Eduardo Kohn's anthropological studies are a great example of this fine-meshed global web of semiotic relations. See Kohn (2013).

[11] Yogi Hendlin comments "What makes interspecies biosemiotics even more exciting—and daunting—for humans is that our task is to understand via our sensorial filters not only the interference pattern of our Umwelt with the Umwelt of another species, but the second-order cross-species meaning-making that occurs between other species' filtered understanding of each other" (2019: 46).

artefact, which only performs under the logic of short-term financial and industrial interests.

According to Hoffmeyer, "The primary mechanism behind semiotic emergence is semiotic scaffolding, the key to nature's tendency to take habits in the biological realm."[12] Considering the dominant, global design culture, what our responses promise are the disruption of semiotic habits for most species. The disappearance of these habits (these species) lead to the "bursts from absence" that Despret speaks about, when the semiotic relations are no-longer present to maintain the stability of ecological patterns. Designing for interdependence involves the re-arrangement, re-composition of environments while attending to the dependencies of multiple beings so that the ecological patterns can be maintained.

In the "Spices-species" project we asked for example, where do the bees that feed on the nectar of passionflowers find shelter when the patterns of the plant species they recognize (the hollow stems of cane, or *Eryngium*) are no-longer present? How could we make carpenter bees interpret the soft cylinders of the set as an opportunity of the environment, an affordance for nesting? Or, in other words, what material triggers could enact "semiotic scaffoldings" to support their ways of being, modes of recognition and increase their capacity for adaptation? The urban context of the city of Córdoba brings its challenges to the carpenter bees we studied. Due to the lack of appreciation or space for the presence of cane or *Eryngium*, which are the plants that these bee species (*Xylocopa artifex* and *Xylocopa ciliata*) recognize, there are longer and longer distances that the bees need to cover to find them. Consulting with specialists we understood that these bees are capable of flying about 500 meters, one reason why our proposition devised a set, what we called a "cycle initiator," that can encourage the growth of the plants even on balconies in the city centre. If the patterns the bees seek are not identifiable, it becomes difficult or impossible for these types of ecological phenomena to occur, thus the project worked with these disrupted links in the semiosphere.

[12] Hoffmeyer (2008b: 156).

## PARTIAL CONNECTIONS

Considering the design interventions that we have been describing as scaffolding, these are, more particularly, the scaffolding of the specific shared interests that overlap in the semiosphere, this overlap is what Donna Haraway and anthropologist Marylin Strathern call *partial connections*. In dialogue, Haraway and Strathern developed the concept of partial connections, which emerges from thinking relationally, in the words of anthropologist Marisol De La Cadena, it offers,

> [. . .] the possibility of conceptualizing entities (or collectives) *with* relation integrally implied, thus disrupting them as units; emerging from the relation, entities are intra-related (Barad 2007) instead of being inter-related . . . instead of plurality (a feature premised on units) the mathematical image congenial to partial connections is that of fractals: they offer the possibility of describing irregular bodies that escape Euclidean geometrical measurements because their borders also allow other bodies in—without, however, touching each other everywhere . . . Thus intra-connected, and therefore not units, fractal bodies also resist being divided into "parts and holes" (Strathern 2004), for this is a quality of units.[13]

Through the scaffolding work, as we developed proposals that probed adaptation, we were attempting to identify and cultivate some of the *partial connections* that brought us (some humans and some carpenter bees) together in the overlap, in the crystallization, that became the "cycle initiator." What I am calling "overlap" is namely, a shared attraction to and interest in the flowers of the passionflower, a shared interest in ingesting the plant (for different reasons), and a structure that can hold the growth of the climbing plant that afford nesting for the species *Xylocopa artifex* and *Xylocopa ciliata*, the main pollinators of the plant.

---

[13] Cadena (2015: 32, emphasis in the original).

As such, the artefact we made sought to materialize the *partial connections* of (some) humans: those interested in traditional medicine, those interested in the plant for its fruits, or those who appreciate the beauty of its flowers; and those of (some) nonhumans: the carpenter bees that seek the passionflower for its abundant nectar and pollinate the plants they visit, the butterflies that feed on nectar lay eggs and feed on it as caterpillars, or the birds that feed on its fruits. Some of these overlaps or connections are listed in Figure 4.1.

Returning to the three ecologies with the example of those that relate to the passionflower, it is easier to understand how an "environmental ecology" is enacted and maintained by numberless relations, organic and inorganic. An environmental ecology is dynamically per-formed by the attunement of and to the signs that each species is capable of perceiving through their Umwelten. Through visual and olfactory signs, humans may be attracted to the passionflower, as bees and others are, but unlike the bees,

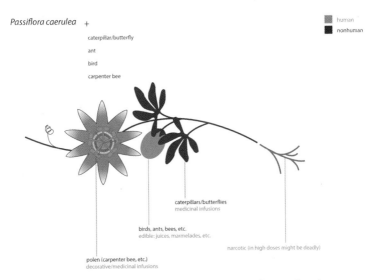

FIGURE 4.1  A few overlaps of interests among those who choose or are chosen by *Passiflora caerulea*. (Illustration by author)

and partially connected to some birds, we prefer (are capable) to feed on its fruits. Unlike other species, we have developed technologies that make possible the more selective extraction of some of the plant's chemicals by producing what we call tinctures. Every interaction makes a difference to those involved in these transactions, affecting and enacting an environmental ecology, in its myriad intersections with the psychological and social ecologies of all participants. There are partial connections emerging from the intersections of the three ecologies, all of them materially entangled, making differences for some-one, for some-thing, some-how.[14]

How could we, by (de)signing, become able to articulate this triple overlapping of the three ecologies? (De)signing not only "produces" signs but is traversed by them, the mental ecology to which I have been mostly discussing as a "psychological ecology" is an ecology that traverses the subjective human dimensions overlapping on the environmental and social ecologics,[15] formed not only by humans but by all that enact the biosphere. In jungles and old forests where the histories of species have co-adapted through tighter and tighter attunement to ecological and semiotic niches, each species' traces are an opportunity for behaviour for some. Working explicitly in this way (to achieve tighter and tighter attunement), is a step to articulate the triple ecological registers of designing.

Returning to "spices-species", what other (de)signing were we performing by inscribing the partitions of this devising? Hoffmeyer states:

> [. . .] the semiosphere poses constraints and boundary conditions upon the Umwelts of various species populations, since

[14] For an earlier version of this argument, see Ávila (2019).

[15] The "mental ecology" sketched by Guattari in 1989, and earlier on by Bateson in 1972 (2000 [1972]) prefigured fields of study such as Ecopsychology, which have emerged at the end of the twentieth century and continue to grow through political ecological studies of different kinds, including decolonial studies. See for example Roszak, Gomes, and Kanner (1995); Abram (1996) and Detraz (2017).

each are forced to occupy specific semiotic niches, which is to say that each will have to master different sets of visual, acoustic, olfactory, tactile and chemical signs in order to survive in the semiosphere. It is thus entirely possible that the semiotic demands made upon species' populations are often a decisive challenge to their success. If this is so, then ecosystem dynamics, for example, shall have to include a proper understanding of the semiotic networks operative in ecosystems.[16]

What other clues would be "operative" in these semiotic networks? The colour of the device? Olfactory signals coming from the materials? The expression of forms? Did the device arrange too much exposure making bees vulnerable to predators or diseases?

Naturecultures demand tuning into different forms of knowledge,[17] and difference in ways of knowing is a challenge as well as a potential asset for maintaining the capability of diversity. A diversity to be appreciated, not only in terms of quantities of species, but also in the diverging interests of each species enacting biodiversity, and thus even in intra-specific terms through the individuals of those species, human and other-than-human. While challenged to tune into multiple knowledges, no project can encompass all, each device will include some and exclude others.

## WHOSE KNOWLEDGE, WHAT KNOWLEDGE, FOR WHOM?

Throughout "Spices-species", we intended to make explicit the possibility not only of growing the plants as (useful and beautiful) companions to humans, but also the possibility of hosting or helping to nurture a few other beings that relate to

[16] Hoffmeyer (2008b: 154).
[17] These questions have long traditions in anthropology. In relation to biodiversity see Escobar (1998). Also, Gutiérrez Borrero (2021).

the plant and participate in the enaction of local ecologies. Historical and geographical aspects influence how people may become able and cultivate predispositions to maintain relations with specific plants and animals. In the particular case of the human population of the province of Córdoba, a region formed by the historical influx of (mostly) European immigrants, the cultural hybridity repeats colonial patterns found in many other parts of the world: "color" as the deviation from the ("white") norm, and indigenous knowledge as naïve and archaic in relation to scientific knowledge. Questioning these, the proposal in its alterity sought to engage in the potential to affirm multiple onto-epistemological approaches that enrich and diversify, supporting the knowledges of those that practice "alternative medicine."

We paid attention to the dynamic aspects (physical and material) of the places, but also, and beyond their geographical location, to the geopolitical, differentiating environment from world, and worlds from worlds. The knowledge derived from indigenous and mestizo or "criollo" cultures and their hybrid cosmologies are partly based on the ecological knowledge of the hilly landscapes (las sierras) in the region. Our work focused on the urban context of the city of Córdoba, also surrounded by the sierras, and influenced by the knowledge and worldviews of those that practice "alternative medicine."

As mentioned, and despite recent legal measures to combat deforestation, only 3–5% of the native forests are left in the region of Córdoba. The knowledge of plants that has been collected by experimentation over centuries by people living in intimate association with their environment is disappearing, with the consequence of silencing these cosmologies, leaving scientific knowledge, not only as dominant but also as the only epistemological register. In spite of progress in synthetic chemistry, 25% of prescription medicines are still derived either directly or indirectly from plants. At the same time, about 80% of the world's population relies on plants for primary health care.[18]

[18] Barboza, G. et al. (2009).

This is important for at least two reasons; it implies the presence and the liveliness of diverse human ways of knowing and relating to the world. It is also important because it indicates that the majority of the human population practices and lives by compound belief systems that vary in degrees, and that each approach validates knowledge that enacts different socio-ecological possibilities. However, because the disappearance of these plants and the human knowledge about them continues to happen, "accelerated acculturation is disintegrating ethnopharmacological information often faster in many areas than the extinction of plant species, which rampant deforestation invariably entails."[19] This advances allopathic medicine with its characteristic detachment from the sources (plants and their habitats), which does not contribute to their knowledge and appreciation, even less towards the knowledge and appreciation of their ecological interdependencies with other beings.

Besides inquiring about human knowledge of these plants and their uses for edible and medicinal purposes, we posed questions about the knowledge of carpenter bees, that helped us shape the artefact by paying attention to them, we asked: How does this species of bee seek and select the most appropriate hollow wood for nesting? What are the perceptive clues that the bees seek? (See Figure 4.2.) Knowing that the female offspring return to the place where they were born for nesting when adults, we asked: Is the artefact long-lasting or able to acknowledge this need somehow? The "cycle initiator" recognizes through its configuration these as well as other questions that helped us shape the artefact. Once we acknowledged and studied the presence of other beings with different perceptual and behavioural capacities, the potential shapes and the potential processes for the implementation and materialization of the devices changed. The signs that we could interpret and be affected by not always led to the possibility of creating what we understood to be partial connections with other creatures, and this informed the design process.

[19] See Barboza, G. et al. (2009).

FIGURE 4.2  Carpenter bee circumnavigating a cane, landing occasionally on its stalk, assessing the suitability of the plant for nesting.
(Illustration based on photograph by Mariano Lucia)

In Figure 4.2 we can see the way a carpenter bee recognizes
the cane, going around to assess the suitability of the cane for a
nest. However, when I asked biologists to explain what exactly
the bee was doing, they were not certain. We still know too little
about this process of recognition, for example, the bee taps on
the surface of the cane occasionally, but it is not known what
kind of information is retrieving. Our proposal has cylindrical
components, so that bees can recognise the patterns of cylindrical
structures and match part of the naturecultures they navigate.
Yet, we cannot say with certainty to what extent or to what degree
this composition can become adopted and provide scaffolding
to the habits that they have developed.

Through the "cycle initiator" we also challenged the most
traditional way by which the passionflower is used as a medicinal
plant. Usually, people that practice alternative medicine take the
parts of the plant to make the infusions that they drink. However,

through the device, by means of the flask that is part of the set, we suggested the production of tinctures instead of infusions since, consulting experts during the research process, it became evident that the chemical properties of the plant were better preserved in this way. By means of adding instructions to make tinctures, it was possible to spare more of the plant and produce more efficient medicine. The preservation of parts of the plant also creates the opportunity for butterflies to feed, or at least the opportunity for those humans that care for the plant to engage with other species that visit it. In this sense, the efforts to design these artefacts may be understood as care in their life-affirming search, and as ecologies of practice that have the potential to maintain caring and develop new sensitivities and relations. Moreover, the overlap in this particular "intersection" human-plant-bee-soil through this material configuration leads to engaging with other tensions than the more common human-plant relations and human-plant-soil relations. By proposing living in proximity to carpenter bees, tension is likely to be part of the relations since many perceive these bees as intimidating due to their size, something that alters the perception of all of them (an aggregate that is greater than the sum of its parts), and which may expand the adaptive capabilities of all species involved.

"Spices-species" does not propose a model of production of this artefact that will demand materials be taken from places that are shadowed, on the contrary, it proposes a responsible use and understanding of local materials and species and a reestablishment of affective bonds; a de-linking from "growth" and a re-linking to the processes of living and dying.

In this context "sustainable development" is not a contradictory expression (since development does not imply expansion), but an expression that emphasises the dynamic aspects and the interrelation between the two words: sustaining (create, test, and maintain adaptive capability) development (create, test, and maintain opportunity).[20] In the context of design, this is how the word "development" may still be realistic in an ecological sense,

[20] Holling and Gunderson (2002).

by acknowledging the dynamic aspects of adaptation, its role in maintaining opportunities for human and other-than-human species.

More specifically, the micropolitical frame of this project implies that both words, sustainment and development, should also be anchored on multiple *anthropos*, and acknowledge partial connections of human cosmologies and ways of knowing. Through the proposed medicinal use, the project suggests a de-linking from (not to replace but to complement) allopathic ways of knowing and the industry of synthetic chemistry that disconnect us at multiple scales from the biomes that we inhabit. The project suggests, in short, an everyday material device that in its commonplace pushes on two levels for "a reworking of the geo- and bio-graphic politics of knowledge."[21] A shift in geo-graphic politics of knowledge through the tensions between global pharmaceutical allopathic industries, and local "traditional" medicinal practices anchored on relational and experiential knowledge of a place; and a shift in bio-graphic politics of knowledge, through the possibility of becoming affected by caring in relation to other-than-humans, enacting alternative ecologies of practice and alternative ecologies of knowledges.

For a human user of this artefact, there are psychological (overlapping social and environmental) tensions through the relations with the plant. By engaging with the maintenance of the plant, the food, and medicine that it may provide to us, our appreciation of its beauty (ugliness, growth, decay), our apprehension or appreciation of the relation with the bees or the feeding on the plant by the caterpillars. Regardless of the number of issues that the artefact manages to respond to, from a human perspective, and rather than emphasizing cultural diversity, the project stresses how different modes of human understanding lead to the enactment of different worlds, in this example through the value systems that result in the contrasts between allopathic medicine and "alternative" medicine, and their ecological implications if care for the plant and species that relate to them are taken into account.

[21] See Mignolo (2011: 123).

## APPROPRIATION THROUGH POLLUTION[22]

Striving to develop devices that perform human responses as responses co-inspired by and for myriad species, cohabitation imposes constraints and imposes demands. One such compromise is exemplified by the encounter of scorpions with humans in bathrooms in the city of Córdoba. As explained in Chapter 2, the way chemicals are currently being disseminated imply a disconnection to the places we live in, and a form of abstraction maintained by the devices we use.

In his book *Malfeasance*, philosopher Michel Serres offers the idea that among living species appropriation of territories takes place through "pollution." Through flushing away our bodily excretions (blood, faeces, semen, urine . . .), we as humans have historically marked and appropriated territory, in a practice common to all living beings. With modernist and centralized network infrastructure, the way we co-create urban ecologies has shifted; disseminating bodily substances through sewage systems which no longer mark a territory or habitat in a concrete form, the system produces a disconnection between our bodies and the territories we live in, increasing abstraction. The network operates to separate us from direct contact with the waste, the excretions, and their encounters with other places and beings as they are flushed away from our homes. In this way, we appropriate local and regional ecosystems by the dissemination of toxins that our household effluents contain, not to mention all the other biophysical processes and materials that have been extracted to build and maintain the infrastructure that leads water from afar into the city to create and re-create our sanitized ordered home (what some term our "ecological footprint").

[22] The sections "Appropriation through pollution" as well as "Realms of exposure" in this chapter, both dedicated to understanding aspects of the grating for scorpions, are based on an earlier publication in collaboration with Henrik Ernstson entitled "Realms of Exposure: On Design, Material Agency and Political Ecologies in Córdoba." In Ernstson and Sörlin (2019).

Design activities (regardless of whether they are performed by professional designers or not) are practices of inscription, where a state of knowledge is applied to deal with an identified situation at a given moment, it follows that the act of inscription creates in turn "partitions" through the creation of a *device*. Using the sewage system as an example, we can consider how the pipelines arrange an inside-outside of their membranes and how these optimize the channelling of flows from the home (or other human-made buildings) to an uncertain location where the effluents are expelled and eventually "treated." The entry and exit points (of waste, water, air, etc.) of the pipeline become opportunities for the entry and exit of many other beings and substances. If when we designed the car, we not only created a way to transport something from A to B, but also the car crash, or at a more global scale, peak-oil and increased $CO_2$ in the atmosphere, by building our sewers we have created not only the possibility to discard unwanted effluents, but also habitats for other life forms, many of them unwanted and unconsidered in the original plan.

The processes by which these devices are materialized, used, and discarded, create arrangements and inscriptions that codify—in and through the systems and environments affected—potential for inclusion and exclusion at different scales. Current material arrangements not only allow for scorpions to multiply, but also, because the installed household gratings (often made of metal alloys) have a fixity or permanence to the sewers, the gratings seem to encourage humans to discharge toxic effluents into them in order to kill the scorpions and, alongside them, a variety of other beings. Although there are new accessories, thinner meshes, that prevent scorpions from passing through conventional gratings, these do not change the perception of "who is there" and "who and what is valuable" in the city.

Counteracting these partitions, the device that we proposed attempted to enact an alternative affective ecology and a different configuration of the political assembly by including other-than-human "voices." Michel Serres helps us to sketch out the wider and seldom-visible ontological dimensions of urban ecologies, here viewed as those relations enacted when species meet and interact, and how their modes of being are rubbed up against each other. In this case, rubbed against each other since scorpions proliferate in the sewers and, by being numerous, threaten to emerge from a shower grating by accident. Humans, on the other hand, poison the water flows where scorpions and many others live, a human appropriation through pollution in abstraction, to which the device we suggested attempts to re-ground by territorializing in concrete, as a physical boundary that acts as a threshold, without further disrupting the lives of those connected to the sewage system, be they scorpion or others. In this way, there is a change of perception, by means of recognition through the device, of "who is there" and "who and what is valuable" in the city.

In this respect Donna Haraway's work can bridge the ontological and the political, acting on her proposition "to become worldly and to respond"; manifested in this case through the use of design, as material responses that evidence our abilities to engage (or not) in and with the life of others, as means to trigger response-ability.

A political dimension is inextricably entangled in and with our modes of being, and intimately connected to our bodies. To this, philosopher Jacques Rancière offers a particular definition of politics that pivots on what can be sensed and felt. Rancière defines the political assembly as a "partition of the sensible," which he views as a particular order that operates in the background to distinguish between speaking-beings, those with speech and voice, and those perceived as simply producing noise. He insists that while there might be a lot of discussion about policies and politics, a "proper political moment" is one that turns around events when those who have no part in the assembly claim their part. When the non-counted are forcing themselves into our community to be recognized, heard, and counted as equals; when the partition of the sensible is disturbed, or disrupted; only then do we have a proper political moment, which necessarily requires a re-configuration of the political assembly.[23]

[23] See Serres (2010); Haraway (2008); Rancière, J. (2010); Meijer (2019).

## AFFECTIVE URBAN ECOLOGIES

The scorpion grating in "Doomestics" aims to enact affective ecologies in several ways. To start with, the darkening surface of the grate shows what is normally imperceptible, namely, the degradation and flow of materials from a building. As such it belongs more to the paradigm of food than to that of household fixtures or appliances. It thus helps us to perceive the material flows that are disseminated to the environment and, perhaps, to sense the scale at which other artefacts degrade and how they influence our habitats. This direct relationship contributes to the possibility of increasing awareness of how the chemicals of hygiene products, cleaning products, and other products used at home influence the environments we inhabit by being disposed into the sewers.

The device seeks to participate in reconfiguring ways to be in the world. It does so by materializing an uncertainty principle, not completely certain of who or what is going to establish contact with, it is conceived to degrade and disseminate organic and inorganic compounds with chemical compositions that are nontoxic to life forms. However, it is important to note that the device, as always, still divides, and organizes an "above" and "below." It does not claim to arrange some kind of flat ontology where all is collaboration and bliss. Rather, it stays with the trouble and tension in trying to maintain a separation, an outside to its own relationality. Thus, the grating may also become a trap for some cockroaches and their predators, the scorpions. This can at first glance be viewed as a problematic example of cohabitation because organisms may be killed, which is not the case with the fine mesh wire recommended by city officials in Córdoba. However, while the official mesh is structured around (total) safety, at the cost of "forgetting" and erasing what lives in the sewage systems, our design stays *with* the tensions of cohabitation as it seeks to participate in rearranging more fundamentally an alternative affective ecology. The routine action to replace the grate after it has disseminated its nutrients, after it has become darker and we feel exposed, brings our human collective life closer to the trouble by relating to the species that threatens us while preventing the possibility of human death (by single individuals of this species of scorpions). Even when the grate may kill individual cockroaches and scorpions, it acknowledges their presence and protects their collectives, their *modus vivendi*[24] and habitat; through its materiality and degrading processes, it reminds humans of the presence of scorpions and others and prescribes a physical relation by needing to replace the grate. As such, the grate also forms an explicit part of the metabolic flow of the city and strives to operate within the notion of *semiotic fitness*, as the relation between the life processes and the energy flow canalized through the system. More plainly put, the alternative grate engages humans and relates them to what is under their feet, creating a connection rather than a disconnection by means of visual and material signs, thereby making us sensitive to ecological interactions that have become invisible through current infra-structure. The device arranges a higher degree of exposure to worlds that we, urban humans, are not normally in contact with.

---

[24] In his article on biosemiotic ethics, Yogi Hendlin explains: "*Modus vivendi* differs from other ethical systems in that it eschews arrangements requiring 'preconceived, philosophically favored standards of fairness or justice', instead pragmatically making due for present participants to live together according to the particularities of current circumstances (Horton 2010: 438). This flexible, updateable, and contingent ethic is conducive for integrating ecologically enmeshed milieus. Such an ethic sustainably arises out of a history of conflict, where the conflicts are not unalterably resolved, but new equilibria are reached and reinvented afresh, allowing all parties enough power to live their lives well. *Modus vivendi* arrangements often get a bad rap, glossed as hopelessly contingent and unstable compared to codified rules (Becker 2005). Yet, even in human systems, sociologists are convinced that human behavior is overwhelmingly guided by informal, dynamic norms and mores rather than adherence to statutes and laws (Bryne 2012; Hird 2009; Thompson 2010). The implicit and affective or non-institutional aspects of ethics should not be dismissed out of hand. An ethics of an interspecies *modus vivendi*, unlike a universal law, works via a living tradition of ecologically-embedded organisms and abiotic processes." (2019: 46).

## REALMS OF EXPOSURE

Through the particularities of Córdoba, we have explored the divisions between the human domestic environment and the "underworld" of sewage. Our work through design has attempted to expose this lack of contact with basic processes that are vital to any ecological niche, including our own, which may involve acts of killing (some) scorpions and cockroaches, while protecting and nurturing the collective of scorpions and other beings through the release of nutrients. This approach is consistent with Haraway's position that asymmetrical multispecies encounters require caring and nurturing, but also, as we just noted, dying and killing:

> We are in a knot of species coshaping one another in layers of reciprocating complexity all the way down. Response and respect are possible only in those knots, with actual animals and people looking back at each other, sticky with all their muddled histories. Appreciation of the complexity is, of course, invited. But more is required too. Figuring what that more might be is the work of situated companion species. It is a question of cosmopolitics, of learning to be "polite" in responsible relation to always asymmetrical living and dying, and nurturing and killing.[25]

Our alternative design is a direct attempt at inserting a device into one of these many knots. As a mundane artefact, it actively participates at various scales along a natural–artificial continuum in the handling of forms of (human) pollution to increase responseability, our human ability to respond to others. By mediating between different realms of exposure, our work attempts to

[25] Haraway (2008: 42). Haraway expands "The problem is actually to understand that human beings do not get a pass on the necessity of killing significant others, who are themselves responding, not just reacting. (. . .) It is not killing that gets us into exterminism, but making beings killable. (. . .) I do not think we can nurture living until we get better at facing killing. But also get better at dying instead of killing." (2008: 80–81).

expose ontological aspects of design (preferences, behaviour, and beliefs taken for granted) with the intention of increasing our participation in processes that might be difficult but are necessary to negotiate while enhancing our awareness of the (inarticulate) interests of more-than-human collectives. The alternative grating can be said to operate at two levels: a micropolitics, practiced at the singular domestic level and coded with intimate feelings of fear and tensions; and potentially a macropolitics, operating on a massive metabolic and mass educational scale if installed in thousands of households. These politics are enacted through the maintenance that the device requires, maintenance that is intentionally inscribed into it and that pushes humans to be part of something seemingly other (the life of sewage systems and scorpions, the areas where our bodily effluents are ultimately disposed of). The processes that lead the artefact to have an expiration date make impossible the strict separation between spheres of dwellings.

Human artefacts (from mass-produced domestic products to large-scale infrastructural networks) repeat the procedure of leaving our traces on every part of the planet, disseminating novel chemical combinations that do not take into account any other being but humans, nor any other being's chemical or metabolic flow. By entering at such quick pace and interrupting local lifecycles, the biosphere fails to process these chemical combinations, which unravels new, unknown, and harmful dynamics for many species, including our own. Performing as a border, the grate we propose mediates these passages between different "worlds" (of the human-home and the scorpion "underworld") and it does so through its material components, with the hope of contributing toward a thinking, sensing, and doing that is life-affirming.

Our speculation on scorpions in peoples' bathrooms has provided an intimate, everyday setting to think about more-than-human political assemblies and their constitution through the daily rhythm of life (and death) in the city. So do the less tense relations with carpenter bees or with fishes in rivers.

## ARTEFACTS AS PROCESS

At a time when ecological crises expose the short-sightedness of various modes of human development, paradigms of design need to be disrupted so that human exposure to other vital realms and species increases. The result would be a greater understanding of the complex ecological interplay in which humans are involved, including relationships that seem undesirable. In the process, we might also reach a more mature stage of reflection in producing the artificial, so that (design) proposals will consider the life cycles of products in relation to multiple beings.

This book has argued for the potential of designing as a poetic practice and a practice of perception by attempting to tune to multiple Umwelten, and in this way enact a poetics of relating. If poetics deals with the processes involved in the production of works, designing as a poetics of relating suggests an ecology of practices that aims at making things for engaging in processes that lead to cross-species sense making. The forms and arts of cohabitation that can be enacted by relating through design in life-affirming ways require more care, attentiveness, and a renewed sense of togetherness. The responses that design enacts through this caring and attentiveness cannot be fully controlled, only nurtured by engaging in the negotiations of cohabiting. The possibility of a poetics and the poetics of possibility based on ecological and ethical potential may result from these approaches. Andreas Weber has written that,

> To be alive is to be full of life. To be full of life includes not only the body, but also subjective experience. To allow ourselves to be full of life, we need a practice of aliveness that goes beyond the abstract objectivity of reason and incorporates the reality of the living organism and its proper emotions. Such an attitude understands reality as a network of relationships, [. . .] The objectivity claimed by this attitude does not convey control, but is built from the courage to let go. For this reason, only this standpoint can be poetic. Poetic objectivity is not esoteric thinking. It is firmly anchored in

reality. This reality, however, is not a place of value-free measuring and counting, but of embodied self-interests. [. . .] Being a body is an irreducible fact and experience. We *are* bodies; we do not *have* bodies (which means that our body is a thing outside the self). We are bodies through a shared metabolism, through unconsciously partaking in the commons of light, air, and water. We *are* because we are with-others.[26]

As human relationships to an ecosystem diminish or get disentangled, so does the capacity to recognize and respect the ecosystem in its inter- and intra-dependencies. Long-term cohabitation depends on pursuing (and maintaining) a multispecies poetics of diversity, one that systematically works to affirm relationality, interdependence. Caring for the way artefacts connect and disconnect, include and exclude, the importance of the design-driven explorations presented here lie in the making explicit how alternative ways of responding to known situations (valuing a plant for its beauty and medicinal use, or the threat of scorpions) may encourage consideration of, and relation to the lives of other-than-humans. Making explicit, at the same time, the natureculture continuum that engages us in living processes and affect us materially, sensually and on an everyday basis.

Artefacts, like ecologies, have to be understood in their dynamism, as processes, as verbs rather than nouns. And they are processes at least in two senses: One, that despite their duration as useful artefacts, whichever these may be, they are constantly becoming in relation to what they encounter, by disseminating chemicals, by reorganizing their molecular structures. Two, that artefacts are always partial responses that require fine tuning, adaptation, regardless of whether they have been designed for humans or others. Can we say that the artefacts presented here are "alter-natives" in a definitive sense? Not really. The artefacts are provisional and partial attempts to tune to the semiosphere. Incompletely, each one of them will require more

[26] Weber (2019: 137).

tuning, co-adaptation, the continuous engagement in the negotiation with many and diverging interests.

What is at stake in naming an artefact an *alter-native*, or in trying to understand an artefact through the notion of alter-natives, is not only that the artefact may stand as an alternative option to a given reality (something that in various degrees all designs do), but that the artefact itself has been conceived to participate locally in some of the relations that maintain the aliveness of the place where it is passing through, even if for a short period of time. What is at stake is a mattering that seeks to compose with some others, to maintain adaptive capability. Yet, a poetics of relating, written in the gerund form, is a process. Rather than work with the capability, or the capacity for adaptation, it works with the art of adaptation, an action that can be learned and must be cultivated. A poetics of relating may emerge from composing with others at the places where we live while attentive to the responses, seeking to learn and keep composing.

# 5    As a mode of closing: Encounters

I'm maintaining the hobby of prepositions. I love them;
I even dream of only speaking of them, with them by them.
I write for, I live with, I go through. I collect words made up
for the sheer pleasure of it. Over the long excursion of my
language, I encounter a word: encounter. En-counter.
*Biogea*, MICHEL SERRES

## GIVING VOICE

Far from closing, this final section opens up to the poetic challenges of designing for interspecies cohabitation. "Giving voice"
to other-than-humans is not to "give" voice but to listen, to sense,
and tune in to other-than-human worlds. Michel Serres reminds
us of the Latin origin of the word encounter, *incontra*, where
"contra" means "against" therefore the "counter" in "encounter"
often signifies impact, collision, commotion and asks: "how to
make this encounter fertile?" Serres, lover of prepositions, asks
later "How can the *against* change into *for* or *with*?"[1] I believe
that this form of generosity can partially be expressed by anchor-
ing our material cultures in the meaningful webs of the semiosphere,
a sense-making across species. The response-ability that design
is, must become a life-affirming, enlivening activity, yet it cannot

---

[1] Serres (2012: 166 and 170).

be conceived as "positive," it has to be understood as paradoxical, pharmacological. In different degrees, with different intensities, devices do *both*: include *and* exclude, nourish *and* poison, create hospitality *and* hostility. For an enlivening culture of etho-ecological dimensions, we should ask: How many are included in our devising? Who benefits from these inclusions/exclusions? What worlds are at stake? The abstract *against* waged by lack of consideration can change into *for* or *with* by response-ability.

Design cultures can acknowledge the presence and the relational modes of other-than-human beings, to expand possibilities for cohabitation and learn new nuances of meaning by attending to the power asymmetries among humans as well as the power asymmetries with and among other-than-humans. In his last book Guattari wrote,

> An ecology of the virtual is thus just as pressing as ecologies of the visible world. And in this regard, poetry, music, the plastic arts, the cinema—particularly in their performance or performative modalities—have an important role to play, with their specific contribution and as a paradigm of reference in new social and analytic practices (psychoanalytic in the broadest sense). Beyond the relation of actualised forces, virtual ecology will not simply attempt to preserve the endangered species of cultural life but equally to engender conditions for the creation and development of unprecedented formations of subjectivity that have never been seen and never felt. This is to say that generalised ecology—or ecosophy—will work as a science of ecosystems, as a bid for political regeneration, and as an ethical, aesthetic and analytic engagement. It will tend to create new systems of valorisation, a new taste for life, a new gentleness.[2]

The monocultures that erase heterogeneity are not only those that we created through certain practices of agriculture, but more generally, those that we created (and still create) by mater-

---

[2] Guattari (1995: 91–92).

ial and anthropocentric practices that acknowledge no other but some human beings. Seeking to create new systems of valorisation, naming something alter-native begs the questions: Is it? How? Where? For whom? The implications need to be unfolded, traced, maintained, and updated. Alter-native is a name, a word for considering artefact relations in particular ways, but as Isabelle Stengers writes,

> Learning to compose will need many names, not a global one, the voices of many peoples, knowledges, and earthly practices. It belongs to a process of multifold creation, the terrible difficulty of which it would be foolish and dangerous to underestimate *but which it would be suicidal to think of as impossible*. There will be no response other than the barbaric if we do not learn to couple together multiple, divergent struggles and engagements in this process of creation, as hesitant and stammering as it may be.[3]

Aiming at cooperation rather than competition could become the drive of co-adaptation yet we devise inclusions and exclusions, and intuitively choose the fish over the fungi, and lovingly the human child over the scorpion. Life is at stake. Naming something alter-native supports framing a poetics of relating, a designing for interdependence which engages with worlds that diverge, to fabricate a gentleness that can relate to vulnerable beings and might help us sense and care for whom and how our worldings matter.

---

[3] Stengers (2015: 50).

# BIBLIOGRAPHY

Abram, D. (1996) *The Spell of the Sensuous. Perception and Language in a More-Than-Human World*. Vintage Books. New York.

Alexander, C. (1977) *A Pattern Language: Towns, Buildings, Construction*. Oxford University Press. Oxford.

Anker, P. (2001) *Imperial Ecology: Environmental Order in the British Empire, 1895–1945*. Harvard University Press. Cambridge and London.

Anker Lenau, T., Orrù, A. M., and Linkola, L. (2018) Biomimicry in the Nordic Countries. (Report for the Nordic Council of Ministers). Available at: http://dx.doi.org/10.6027/10.6027/NA2018-906.

Arnold, C. (2014) Rethinking Sterile: The Hospital Microbiome. Available at: https://www.ncbi.nlm.nih.gov/pmc/articles/PMC4080534/.

Ávila, M. (2012) *Devices. On Hospitality, Hostility and Design*. ArtMonitor. Gothenburg.

Ávila, M. (2017) Ecologizing, Decolonizing: An Artefactual Perspective. No 7: Nordes 2017: Design+Power, Oslo, www.nordes.org.

Ávila, M. (2019) Three Ecologies Diffracted. Intersectionality for Ecological Caring. No 8: Nordes 2019: Who Cares?, Espoo, Finland, www.nordes.org.

Ávila, M. (2020a) (De)sign responses as response diversity. *Biosemiotics*, 13(1): 41–62. DOI: 10.1007/s12304-019-09374-8

Ávila, M. (2020b) Togetherness. In *Designing in Dark Times: An Arendtian Lexicon*. Staszowski, E. and Tassinari, V. (Eds.). Pp. 306–309. Bloomsbury. New York.

Ávila, M. and Ernstson, H. 2019 Realms of Exposure: On Design, Material Agency and Political Ecologies in Córdoba. In *Grounding Urban Natures: Histories and Futures of Urban Ecologies*. Ernstson, H. and Sörlin, S. (Eds.). Pp. 137–166. MIT Press. Cambridge, Massachusetts.

Barad, K. (2007) *Meeting the Universe Halfway. Quantum Physics and the Entanglement of Matter and Meaning*. Duke University Press. Durham and London.

Barboza, G. E., Cantero, J. J., Núñez, C., Pacciaroni, A., and Ariza Espinar, L. (2009) Medicinal Plants: A General Review and a Phytochemical and Ethnopharmacological Screening of the Native Argentine Flora. *Kurtziana* 34(1–2): Jan/Dec. Available at: http://www.scielo.org.ar/scielo.php?pid=S1852-59622009000100002&script=sci_arttext&tlng=pt

Bateson, G. (2000) [1972] *Steps to an Ecology of Mind*. University of Chicago Press. Chicago.

Bateson, G. (2002) [1979] *Mind and Nature. A Necessary Unity*. Hampton Press. New Jersey.

Bennett, J. (2010) *Vibrant Matter. A Political Ecology of Things*. Duke University Press. Durham and London.

Benyus, J. M. (1997) *Biomimicry: Innovation Inspired by Nature*. Morrow. New York.

Bijker, W. E. and Law, J. (Eds.) (1992) *Shaping Technology/Building Society. Studies in Sociotechnical Change*. MIT Press. Cambridge, Massachusetts.

Blaser, M. and Cadena, M. De La. (2017) The Uncommons: An Introduction. *Anthropologica* 59: 191–192.

Boehnert, J. (2015) Ecological Literacy in Design Education. A Theoretical Introduction. In *Form Akademisk*. 8(1): 1–11. Available at: https://journals.oslomet.no/index.php/form-akademisk/issue/view/68.

Boehnert, J. (2018) *Design, Ecology, Politics: Towards the Ecocene*. Bloomsbury. London and New York.

Bonsiepe, G. (2021) *The Disobedience of Design*. Bloomsbury. London.

Braidotti, R. (2013) *The Posthuman*. Polity Press. Cambridge.

Butler, J. (2011) Precarious Life and The Obligations of Cohabitation. Available at: https://www.terada.ca/discourse/wp-content/uploads/2012/06/Butler_Sweden2011.pdf.

Cadena, M. De La. (2015) *Earth Beings. Ecologies of Practice Across Andean Worlds*. Duke University Press. Durham and London.

Cadena, M. De La. (2019) Uncommoning Nature: Stories from the Anthropo-not-seen. In *Anthropos and the Material*. Harvey, P., Krohn-Hansen, C., and Nustad, K. G. Duke University Press. Durham and London.

Davidson-Hunt, I. J., Turner, K. L., Pareake Mead, A. T., Cabrera-Lopez, J., Bolton, R., Idrobo, C. J., Miretski, I., Morrison, A. and Robson, J. P. (2012) Biocultural Design: A New Conceptual Framework for Sustainable Development in Rural Indigenous and Local Communities. *S.A.P.I.EN.S* [Online], 5(2). Available at: http://sapiens.revues.org/1382.

Deleuze, G. and Guattari, F. (2004) [1980] *A Thousand Plateaus. Capitalism and Schizophrenia*. Continuum. London.

Despret, V. (2016) *What Would Animals Say if We Asked the Right Questions?* Translated by Brett Buchanan. University of Minnesota Press. Minneapolis.

Detraz, N. (2017) *Gender and the Environment*. Polity Press. Cambridge.

Dilnot, C. (2015) The Matter of Design. *Design Philosophy Papers*, 13(2): 115–123.

Dilnot, C. (2021) Designing in the World of the Naturalised Artificial. In *Design in Crisis. New Worlds, Philosophies and Practices*. Fry, T. and Nocek, A. (Eds.). Routledge. London and New York.

Donaldson, S. and Kymlicka, W. (2011) *Zoopolis. A Political Theory of Animal Rights*. Oxford University Press. Oxford and New York.

Dubreuil, L. (2006) Leaving Politics: Bios, Zōē, Life. Translated by C. Eagle. *Diacritics*, 36(2): 83–98.

Dunn, R. (2018) *Never Home Alone: From Microbes to Millipedes, Camel Crickets, and Honeybees, The Natural History of Where We Live*. Basic Books. New York.

Edmundson, W. A. (2015) Do Animals Need Citizenship? *International Journal of Constitutional Law*. 13(3): 749–765. Available at: https://doi.org/10.1093/icon/mov046.

Elands, B.H.M., Vierikko, K., Andersson, E., Fischer, L. K., Gonçalves, P., Haase, D., Kowarik, I., Luz, A. C., Niemelä, J., Santos-Reis, M., and Wiersum, K. F. (2019) Biocultural Diversity: A Novel Concept to assess Human–Nature Interrelations, Nature Conservation and Stewardship in Cities. *Urban Forestry & Urban Greening*. 40: 29–34. Available at: https://doi.org/10.1016/j.ufug.2018.04.006.

Elmqvist, T., Folke, C., Nyström, M., Peterson, G., Bengtsson, J., Walker, B., and Norberg, J. (2003) Response Diversity, Ecosystem Change, and Resilience. *Frontiers in Ecology and the Environment*. 1(9): 488–494. The Ecological Society of America.

Ernstson, H., and Sörlin, S. (Eds.) (2019) *Grounding Urban Natures: Histories and Futures of Urban Ecologies*. MIT Press. Cambridge, Massachusetts.

Ernstson, H., and Swyngedouw, E. (Eds.) (2019) *Urban Political Ecology in the Anthropo-obscene. Interruptions and Possibilities*. Routledge. London.

Escobar, A. (1998) Whose Knowledge, Whose nature? Biodiversity, Conservation, and the Political Ecology of Social Movements. *Journal of Political Ecology*. 5(1): 53–82.

Escobar, A. (2018) *Designs for the Pluriverse*. Duke University Press. Durham and London.

Fallan, K. (Ed.) (2019) *The Culture of Nature in the History of Design*. Routledge. New York.

Gay, A. and Samar, L. (1994) *El Diseño Industrial en la Historia*. Ediciones TEC. Córdoba.

Gilbert, S. F. and Epel, D. (2015) *Ecological Developmental Biology: The Environmental Regulation of Development, Health, and Evolution*. Sinauer Associates. Sunderland.

Glissant, E. (1997) *Poetics of Relation*. Translated by Betsy Wing. University of Michigan Press. Michigan.

Goleman, D., Bennett, L., Barlow, Z. (2012) *Ecoliterate: How Educators Are Cultivating Emotional, Social, and Ecological Intelligence*. Jossey-Bass. San Francisco.

Grosz, E. (2008) *Chaos, Territory, Art. Deleuze and the Framing of the Earth*. Columbia University Press. New York.

Guattari, F. (2008) [1989] *The Three Ecologies*. Continuum. London.

Guattari, F. (1995) [1992] *Chaosmosis*. Indiana University Press. Bloomington.

Gudynas, E. (2014) *Derechos de la Naturaleza. Ética biocéntrica y políticas ambientales*. Available at: http://gudynas.com/wp-content/uploads/GudynasDerechosNaturalezaLima14r.pdf.

Gutiérrez Borrero, A. (2021) *DESSOCONS. Diseños del sur, de los sures, otros, con otros nombres*. Universidad de Caldas. Doctorado en Diseño y Creación. Manizales.

Göransdotter, M. (2020) *Transitional Design Histories*. No. 008. Umeå Institute of Design Research Publications. Umeå, Sweden.

Haraway, D. J. (2003) *The Companion Species Manifesto: Dogs, People, and Significant Otherness*. Prickly Paradigm Press. Chicago

Haraway, D. J. (2008) *When Species Meet*. University of Minnesota Press. Minneapolis.

Haraway, D. J. (2016) *Staying with the Trouble. Making Kin in the Chthulucene*. Duke University Press. Durham and London.

Hendlin, Y. H. (2016) Multiplicity and *Welt. Sign Systems Studies* 44(1/2): 94–110.

Hendlin, Y. H. (2019) Interspecies Signaling and Habituated Conviviality. *Recherches sémiotiques/Semiotic Inquiry*, 39(1/2). Association canadienne de sémiotique/Canadian Semiotic Association.

Hoffmeyer, J. (2008) *Biosemiotics. An Examination into the Life of Signs and the Signs of Life*. University of Scranton Press. Scranton and London.

Hoffmeyer, J. (2008b) Semiotic Scaffolding of Living Systems. In *Introduction to Biosemiotics*. Barbieri, M. (Ed.). Pp. 149–166. Springer Science+Business Media. Dordrecht, Holland.

Hoffmeyer, J. (2015) Introduction: Semiotic Scaffolding. *Biosemiotics.* 8: 153–158.

Hoffmeyer, J. And Emmeche, C. (1991) Code-Duality and the Semiotics of Nature. Retrieved on November 12, 1998 from http://www.nbi.dk/~emmeche/coPubl/91.JHCE/codedual.html. The final version of the paper is published in: *On Semiotic Modeling* Anderson M. and Merrell, F. (Eds.). Pp. 117–166. Mouton de Gruyter. Berlin and New York.

Holling, C. S. and Gunderson, L. H. (Eds.) (2002) *Panarchy. Understanding Transformations in Human and Natural Systems.* Island Press. Washington.

Hoppe, K. (2019) Responding as Composing: Toward a Post-anthropocentric, Feminist Ethics in the Anthropocene. *Distinktion: Journal of Social Theory.* Available at: https://doi.org/10.1080/1600910X.2019.1618360

Hudson, W. H. (2005) [1918] *Far Away and Long Ago. A Childhood in Argentina.* Eland Publishing. London.

Ingold, T. (2000) *The Perception of the Environment: Essays on Livelihood, Dwelling and Skill.* Routledge. London.

Kapsali, V. (2016) *Biomimetics for Designers. Applying Nature's Processes and Materials in The Real World.* Thames & Hudson, New York.

Kohn, E. (2013) *How Forests Think. Toward and Anthropology Beyond the Human.* University of California Press. Berkeley.

Kothari, A., Salleh, A., Escobar, A., Demaria, F., Acosta, A. (Eds.) (2018) *Pluriverse: A Post-Development Dictionary.* Available at: https://degrowth.org/2018/04/14/new-book-pluriverse-a-post-development-dictionary/

Krippendorff, K. (2006) *The Semantic Turn; A New Foundation for Design.* Taylor & Francis. New York.

Kull, K. (2012) Scaffolding. In *A More Developed Sign: Interpreting the Work of Jesper Hoffmeyer.* Favareau, D., Cobley, P. and Kull, K. (Eds.). Pp. 227–230. Tartu Semiotics Library 10. Tartu University Press. Tartu.

Kull, K. (2016) The Biosemiotic Concept of the Species. *Biosemiotics* 9: 61–71.

Latour, B. (1992) Where Are the Missing Masses? The Sociology of a few Mundane Artefacts. In *Shaping Technology/ Building Society. Studies in Sociotechnical Change.* Bijker, W. E. and Law, J. (Eds.). Pp. 225–258. MIT Press. Cambridge, Massachusetts.

Latour, B. (2004) *Politics of Nature*. Harvard University Press. Cambridge.

Latour, B. (2013) *An Inquiry into Modes of Existence*. Harvard University Press. Cambridge.

MacDonough, W. and Braungart, M. (2002) *Cradle to Cradle. Remaking the Way We Make Things*. North Point Press. New York.

Mahler, A. G. (2017) Global South. *Oxford Bibliographies in Literary and Critical Theory*, ed. Eugene O'Brien. Accessed June 21, 2021.

Maran, T. (2020) *Ecosemiotics*. Cambridge University Press. Cambridge.

Maran, T. (2021) The *Ecosemiosphere* is a Grounded Semiosphere. A Lotmanian Conceptualization of Cultural-Ecological Systems. *Biosemiotics*. Available at: https://doi.org/10.1007/s12304-021-09428-w.

Marder, M. (2013) *Plant Thinking. A Philosophy of Vegetal Life*. Columbia University Press. New York.

Margulis, L. (1998) *Symbiotic Planet (A New Look at Evolution)*. Basic Books. New York.

Margulis, L. and Sagan, D. (2007) *Dazzle Gradually: Reflections on the Nature of Nature*. Chelsea Green. Vermont.

Martin, A., Coolsaet, B., Corbera, W., Dawson, N. M., Fraser, J. A., Lehman, I. and Rodriguez, I. (2016) Justice and conservation: The need to incorporate recognition. *Biological Conservation*. 197: 254–261.

Martínez, G. J. (2015) [2010] *Las Plantas en la Medicina Tradicional de las Sierras de Córdoba. Un recorrido por la cultura campesina de Paravachasca y Calamuchita*. Detodoslosmares. Córdoba.

Marx, K. (1981) *Capital*, vol. III. Vintage. New York.

Mathews, F. (2012) The Anguish of Wildlife Ethics. *New Formations* 75: 114–131.

Maturana, H. and Varela, F. (1980) *Autopoiesis and Cognition: The Realization of the Living*. D. Reidel Pub. Co. Dordrecht, Holland.

Maturana, H. and Varela, F. (1998) *The Tree of Knowledge*. Shambhala. Boston and London.

Meijer, E. (2019) *When Animals Speak. Toward an Interspecies Democracy*. New York University Press. New York.

Mignolo, W. D. (2011) *The Darker Side of Western Modernity. Global Futures, Decolonial options*. Duke University Press. Durham and London.

Monbiot, G. (2014) *Feral. Rewilding the Land, Sea and Human Life.* Penguin. London.

Orr, D. (1992) *Ecological Literacy: Education and the Transition to a Postmodern World.* State University of New York Press. Albany.

Orrù, A. M. (2017) *Wild Poethics. Exploring Relational and Embodied Practices in Urban Making.* Chalmers University of Technology. Gothenburg.

Penty, J. (2019) *Product Design and Sustainability: Strategies, Tools, and Practice.* Routledge. New York.

Plumwood, V. (2002) *Environmental Culture. The Ecological Crisis of Reason.* Routledge. New York.

Plumwood, V. (2008) Shadow Places and the Politics of Dwelling. *Australian Ecological Review.* 44: 139–150.

Polis, G.A. (Ed.) (1990) *The Biology of Scorpions.* Stanford University Press. Stanford.

Puig de la Bellacasa, M. (2017) *Matters of Care. Speculative Ethics in More Than Human Worlds.* University of Minnesota Press. Minneapolis and London.

Rancière, J. (2010) *Dissensus: On Politics and Aesthetics.* Bloomsbury. London and New York.

Rancière, J. (2014) *Moments Politiques: Interventions 1977–2009.* Seven Stories Press. New York.

Redström, J. (2017) *Making Design Theory.* MIT Press. Cambridge and London.

Rose, D. B., van Dooren, T., and Churley, M. (2017) *Extinction Studies: Stories of Time, Death, and Generations.* Columbia University Press. New York.

Roszak, T., Gomes, M. E., and Kanner, A. E. (Eds.) (1995) *Ecopsychology. Restoring the Earth, Healing the Mind.* Counterpoint. Berkeley.

Sagan, D. (2011) The Human is More than Human: Interspecies Communities and the New "Facts of Life". Theorizing the Contemporary, *Fieldsights*, November 18. https://culanth.org/fieldsights/the-human-is-more-than-human-interspecies-communities-andthe-new-facts-of-life

Santos, B. S. and Meneses, M. (Eds.) (2014) *Epistemologías del Sur.* Akal. Madrid.

Scarry, E. (1985) *The Body in Pain. The Making and Unmaking of the World.* Oxford University Press. New York and Oxford.

Scarry, E. (1999) *On Beauty and Being Just.* Princeton University Press. Princeton and Oxford.

Schneider, E. D. and Sagan, D. (2005) *Into The Cool. Energy Flow, Thermodynamics and Life*. The University of Chicago Press. Chicago and London.

Serres, M. (2010) *Malfeasance. Appropriation Through Pollution?* Stanford University Press. Stanford.

Serres, M. (2012) *Biogea*. Univocal Publishing. Minneapolis.

Sharma, K. (2015) *Interdependence. Biology and Beyond*. Fordham University Press. New York.

Staszowski, E. and Tassinari, V. (Eds.). (2020) *Designing in Dark Times – An Arendtian Lexicon*. Bloomsbury. New York.

Stengers, I. (2005) Introductory notes on an ecology of practices. *Cultural Studies Review*. 11(1): 183–196.

Stengers, I. (2015) *In Catastrophic Times. Resisting the Coming Barbarism*. Open Humanities Press, London.

Stoknes, P. E. (2015) *What We Think About When We Try not to Think About Global Warming. Toward a New Psychology of Climate Action*. Chelsea Green Publishing. Vermont.

Tsing, A. L. (2017) *The Mushroom at the End of the World*. Princeton University Press. Princeton.

Varela, F. J. (1999) *Ethical Know-How. Action, Wisdom and Cognition*. Stanford University Press. Stanford.

Vernadsky, V. I. (1997) [1926] *The Biosphere*. Copernicus. Springer-Verlag. New York.

Viveiros de Castro, E. (2014) *Cannibal Metaphysics*. University of Minnesota Press. Minneapolis.

Von Uexküll, J. (2001) An Introduction to Umwelt. *Semiotica* 134(1/4): 107–110.

Von Uexküll, J. (2010) *A Foray Into the World of Animals and Humans*. University of Minnesota Press. Minneapolis and London.

Watkin, C. (2020) *Michel Serres. Figures of Thought*. Edinburgh University Press. Edinburgh.

Watson, J. (2020) *Lo–Tek: Design by Radical Indigenism*. Taschen. Berlin and New York.

Weber, A. (2019) *Enlivenment: Toward a Poetics for the Anthropocene*. MIT Press. Cambridge, Massachusetts.

Weber, A. (2017) *Matter and Desire: An Erotic Ecology*. Chelsea Green Publishing. White River Junction.

Wheeler, W. (2016) *Expecting the Earth. Life, Culture, Biosemiotics*. Lawrence & Wishart. London.

Wilson, E. O. (2016) *Half-Earth. Our Planet Fight for Life*. Liveright Publishing. New York.

Whitener, B. (2018) Animal accumulation. *Blind Field Journal*. Available at: https://blindfieldjournal.com/2018/08/04/animal-accumulation/.

Yusoff, K. (2018) *A Billion Black Anthropocenes or None*. University of Minnesota Press. Minneapolis.

Zaffaroni, E. R. (2015) *La Pachamama y el Humano*. Ediciones Madres de Plaza de Mayo. Buenos Aires.

# INDEX

Page numbers in **bold** refer to figures.